EAST AFRICAN JOURNEYS

by BRIAN B HARVEY

Balboa Press books may be ordered through booksellers or by contacting:

Balboa Press
A Division of Hay House
1663 Liberty Drive
Bloomington, IN 47403
www.balboapress.co.uk
UK TFN: 0800 0148647 (Toll Free inside the UK)
UK Local: 02036 956325 (+44 20 3695 6325 from outside the UK)

ISBN: 978-1-9822-8228-8 (sc)
ISBN: 978-1-9822-8229-5 (e)

Print information available on the last page.

Balboa Press rev. date: 10/09/2020

BALBOA.PRESS
A DIVISION OF HAY HOUSE

DEDICATION

To my darling Jan who has been my constant travel
companion and my inspiration for travelling.

PREFACE

What makes travelling so interesting, so intriguing and so compulsive? What is it that makes you want to explore new parts of the world and never feel you have seen enough? We talk about a travel bug, and that is just what it is, an infection for which the only cure is to continue travelling. It may be an innate feeling or it may creep up on you after a cultural experience, but once you have it, you always want more. That is the same effect as any drug, but the wonderful thing is that there is no downside.

Over the years my wife and I had previously travelled, but our ventures were usually within Europe. This was because we owned a touring caravan and Europe was our limit. It was not only limited in area but also culturally, because Europe is culturally similar wherever you go. There may be differences in language but the countries of Europe are not basically different from each other.

What started us seeking the world came later in life when we were nearly in our sixties. It started when our son Duncan joined VSO and invited us to visit him in his first posting, Eritrea. We did not even know where that was and had to look on a map to find it. But ultimately we found that journey absolutely enthralling. It set the travel bug within us buzzing and it made us want to travel more and more and to experience other cultures. It became the start of our later travels throughout the world. What is even more interesting is that we started at an age when many people might be contemplating retiring yet we discovered that provided you remain reasonably fit you can carry on travelling without fear at any age. We had previously been under the impression that it was prohibitively expensive, and it probably is if you need agents to make all your arrangements for you. Yet it is so easy to make your own decisions and travel independently if you use the resources available to you. At the time of our starting our "bible" was the Lonely Planet Guide series. Later, with the introduction of the internet it is even easier, although the Guides still give you greater insight. Independent travel also brings you in touch with local people which you could never achieve travelling in a tour group. We travelled as backpackers and entered a world of young travellers who had the same inclinations as us; the only difference was our age. At first we were reluctant to impose in any way on these youngsters who were of a similar age to our own children, but strangely they often wanted to talk to us to ask why we were travelling at our age. Many times we had the comment that they wished their parents would do what we were doing which invited us to ask them why they did not. But I am getting ahead of myself.

This volume concentrates on our visits to Eastern Africa where we entered a world we had not previously envisaged and saw life, sometimes in the raw. The story of Eritrea is an absolute tragedy because, for us, it started with our admiration for a people who had undergone grave hardships through a civil war, but who were working hard to rebuild their nation. It ended with yet another war and ultimately with a people being oppressed by a dictator who was trying to enslave his people, causing mass exodus for those brave enough to avoid detection and leave.

But this is real life, not some romantic tale. It is probable that these situations are repeated elsewhere, but the trick is to get there before the problems start. We were very lucky to be in Eritrea at what was for them a golden period before the disappointment set in. We can never forget the experiences we had there, the kindness of the people and the strength of character they displayed. This was in stark contrast to our expectations before we arrived there for the first time.

Having tasted a culture that was so different from any we had experienced we set our sights on travelling to every corner of the world. This East African volume describes how it started and continued.

EAST AFRICAN JOURNEYS
ERITREA

At the end of August 1996 I went with my wife Jan to visit our son Duncan who had been working in Eritrea for a year as a Voluntary Service Overseas (VSO) volunteer. It was to be the most moving four weeks of our lives and an experience we will never forget. Duncan was half way through a two year tour and was working as an English teacher in a remote village in the south. He had been writing to us regularly during his first year and we had learned a lot about his way of life in the village and the friends he had made. The most significant aspect we learned was the fact that Eritreans had so little but were striving to achieve so much. A little over 5 years after the end of their most disastrous civil war with Ethiopia they were doing all they could to rebuild the country. What was this war about and why were they so determined to succeed? To answer these questions I must give you some background information and tell you a little about their history.

Eritrea is an old name but a newly formed independent country in the North East corner of Africa. It is about the size of England and lies on the Red Sea coast with Sudan to the north and west and Ethiopia to the south. The name dates back to Roman times but the boundaries of the country itself were formed by the Italians in the era of the "Scramble for Africa" from 1894 to the early part of the 20th century. In this period the Italians built much of its infrastructure including the capital Asmara with its long palm-fringed avenues, the beautiful port of Massawa on the Red Sea and also created roads which spanned the length and breadth of the country and a railway linking some of the main towns. The Italians controlled the country right up to 1941, when they were driven out by British forces during the Second World War. An apparently reluctant British regime lasted until December 1950 when by a United Nations resolution Eritrea was federated as an autonomous unit with Ethiopia.

This turned out to be a disastrous decision because from the beginning Ethiopia treated Eritrea as a subjugated territory and instead of providing Governors with Eritrean background; the first three were all sons-in-law of Haile Selassie, the Ethiopian Emperor. A policy of creeping control was adopted and gradually Eritrean officials were replaced by Ethiopians, then the main languages of Eritrea, Tigrinya and Arabic, were barred as the official languages used in schools and were replaced by Amharic, the main Ethiopian language. This led to student boycotts and protests by officials and in the workplace was met by an increase in police brutality. A number of industries were closed and transferred to Ethiopia as part of a process of undermining the economic independence of Eritrea. In 1958 there was a General Strike which was brutally suppressed with many killed and wounded, after which Eritrea tried to appeal to the United Nations but was not allowed into the United Nations Assembly. Eventually armed struggle was seen as the only solution and this started in September 1961 which led to Ethiopia virtually dissolving the Eritrean assembly and annexing the country.

What followed was 30 years of guerrilla fighting which incredibly received very little publicity in the West. In 1974 Haile Selassie was deposed and replaced by a Communist regime under President Mengistu whose regime intensified the barbarity of the control in Eritrea. Many important Eritrean officials were arrested and executed without trial including two previous prime ministers. This led to increased resistance and in 1977, just when the Eritreans were on the point of winning their struggle for independence, Mengistu's forces were bolstered by massive cash and arms aid from the Soviet Union. This aid enabled Mengistu to regain and strengthen his control over Eritrea. The coming of Mengistu also affected Ethiopia itself for he introduced a Land Reform Bill in 1975 which outlawed the private ownership of land, and initiated collective land use under the control of local councils. This was badly administered and led to widespread famine in later years. In the early 1980s the situation was complicated in Ethiopia by a series of harvest failures due to the rains not coming for three successive years. This led to famine which in turn caused unrest in Ethiopia. Mengistu tried to pull the country back into some sort of order, as much as anything by arresting and killing opposition leaders and driving into exile those who survived his purges. Thousands upon thousands of Ethiopians were killed by the army and many thousands more fled from the killing and the famine.

Who can forget what we saw on TV in the early 1980's when the terrible plight of the refugees fleeing from the war, coupled with failed harvests led to mass starvation? This prompted a huge humanitarian response from Western Countries prompted by the distressing sights we saw daily on our screens and by the promptings of Bob Geldof who started "Live Aid", which raised millions of pounds and worked in conjunction with the many relief agencies. But Mengistu's unwillingness to allow aid to the worst affected province in the North East (bordering Eritrea) exacerbated the situation and led to more than 1 million Ethiopian deaths.

The end of the Mengistu regime started with the collapse of the Soviet Union in 1990. Reduced military aid led to his weakened army being driven from Eritrea and even the North East of Ethiopia which was by now in open rebellion. During May 1991, Eritrea finally completed the liberation of their country by taking the capital Asmara. At the same time Ethiopian rebel troops were taking the Ethiopian capital Addis Ababa and Mengistu jetted to safety to Zimbabwe. The new government abandoned the failed Socialist policies and co-operated in the setting up of a transitional government in Eritrea. In May 1993 Eritrea held a referendum to finally decide on independence from Ethiopia and 99.81% of the population voted for independence. On 24 May 1993 this was formally declared and a leading fighter in the struggle, Isaias Afwerki, was declared the country's President.

Eritrea was left devastated by the 30 years of war and the process of national reconstruction was an enormous one. Massawa, the main port on the Red Sea, through which most trade was conducted, was virtually destroyed and many of the main towns were severely damaged. Only the capital Asmara survived largely intact due to the fact that no serious fighting had occurred there. The total railway system was destroyed and most of the main roads were in need of significant repair. Housing was also a severe problem. This was the situation which President Afwerki faced in 1993, with a population estimated to be about 3.5 million with a further 500,000 refugees in Sudan and 200,000 exiles in various parts of the world. Characteristically he was able to mobilise the people to a massive effort of reconstruction, much of it voluntary. The priorities were re-establishing agriculture, industry and communications whilst education was seen as a significant part of the renewal for without it his people could not hope to survive in the modern world.

There are nine ethnic groups in Eritrea each with their own languages and although Tigrinya and Arabic are the main languages there is not an official language. In fact President Afwerki has been astute in ensuring that no ethnic group or culture is seen as predominating, especially since the war had been fought largely because of the attempts by Ethiopia to suppress all ethnic culture. Italian is also spoken, especially by the older generation, but English is seen as the key language to use in all Eritrea's dealings with the outside world. In all schools English is the teaching language from Grade 7 onwards (the equivalent of secondary level education). That means that every subject from grade 7 is conducted in a foreign language!

This is where Duncan comes in for through the agency of VSO he was employed by the Eritrean government as an English teacher. There is a grave shortage of teachers in the country and this presents many problems. Inevitably class sizes are large and the age range in each varies considerably due to the fact that every student must pass exams at each level before he or she can progress to the next level. As many young people were denied any education during "the struggle", as it is widely referred to, it is common to find people of up to age 25 in any class trying to catch up on lost time. This leads to a high school population and as a consequence many children are unable to receive an education because the schools are full.

With this knowledge we had set out to visit Duncan, flying direct from Heathrow to Asmara. Although we knew a lot about the people in Duncan's village, we wondered just what these people who had waged a 30 year war and had undergone such privations would be like. Would they be difficult, surly or just plain tough? We were about to find out. It was early in the morning and also the rainy season so it was no surprise to find as we approached the airport that it was shrouded in heavy cloud. I should explain that Asmara is situated on a high plateau which encompasses most of central Eritrea, at an altitude of more than 7000 feet so the cloud was to be expected. What we hadn't expected was that the large 737 jet would start to descend then suddenly roar off without landing. The pilot explained that he couldn't see the runway but would try again. We were all anxious at this news but were relieved that on the second attempt the runway was visible and we landed without mishap.

We had arrived, and on entering the terminal building we looked around to get some first impressions. What greeted us looked like a building site with workmen everywhere busily routing cables, painting and drilling with great curtains of polythene covering large areas. We joined a long queue at the immigration desk which moved forward very slowly indeed. After about an hour it was our turn to show our passports, visas and landing cards and it was here that we got our first inkling of what the Eritrean people were like. Immigration officials the world over are particularly taciturn and severe people so it was with some surprise that we were greeted by the man with a big smile and "Welcome to our country". He examined our cards thoroughly and said "Oh I see you are going to stay in Tera Emni (Duncan's village) such a pretty village, I know it well". Then he handed all our papers back and said as he did so "100%". We returned his smile, thanked him and moved on but it was only later that the significance of his remark dawned on us. He had not needed to complete or correct our landing cards, a task he had been doing very patiently for many of the others who had been ahead of us in the long queue and also explained why we had been waiting so long. We were greatly impressed.

Only travellers are permitted into the airport terminal so we had to wait until we got outside before we met Duncan. It was an emotional greeting and we just stood and chatted for some time. He looked very well indeed, he was tanned and had put on a little weight but curiously had developed a lilt to his speech. We were to realise later that he had worked extremely hard at learning Tigrinya, and he now spoke it very well indeed which had the effect of colouring his speech. We then got a taxi and travelled the 5 miles into the centre of Asmara. On the way we saw evidence of the extent of the rebuilding that is on-going, with rows of three-storey western type flats under construction. We were to realise that this was not typical of the dwellings in Eritrea and must be something of a new departure to ease the housing problem, for a typical house was often a square shaped single storied flat roofed building. The entry into the city was along a dual carriageway, fringed with palm trees and looking very Italian with many beautiful buildings. Our hotel, one of the best in Asmara, looked so from the outside but inside was somewhat in need of renovation, but the room was comfortable and clean with an en suite shower which was already confounding our worst expectations.

We settled in quite quickly and having found a convenient bank to change my money into Birr, the local currency (there are almost 10 Birr to the pound so calculating values was easy) we went to the large Asmaran market. We only went to see the sights as we did not need to purchase anything and we were not disappointed. There were stalls which sold fruit and vegetables and there were marvellous aromatic spices, but here live animals were on sale - to eat! The average Eritrean, even those who lived in the capital could not afford refrigeration so meat is purchased live, killed and eaten within three days and any residual meat is dried for longer preservation. Families frequently join together to make such purchases and so there were sheep, goats and chickens in abundance. Clothing could be purchased but the quality was not very good as this is still a cottage industry in the emerging Eritrea and the same applied to the artifacts which were on sale. Virtually everything was hand-made and often from recycled materials. For instance you could buy small tin trunks with lockable lids entirely refashioned from large tin cans which had been cut and skillfully reshaped and brightly painted with local designs. We subsequently found these in many homes we visited and served as the equivalent of cupboards for food storage. There was not a single item for sale which one might term a tourist item. Everything was practical and for use in any Eritrean home.

Duncan knew some of the traders and stopped to chat with them and we became aware just how much of the language he had picked up. We, being the only white faces around, attracted much interest and we were asked many questions, via Duncan. The most frequently asked question and the one which everyone was most interested to hear was "Did we like Eritrea". They seemed to place so much importance on the answer and were pleased with the affirmative response we invariably gave despite the fact that we had only just arrived. This was to happen repeatedly in our travels and it made us realise that they wanted outsiders to appreciate the efforts the whole country was making to rebuild.

After this visit we went to have lunch at one of Duncan's favourite cafes. He helped us by describing the menu (which was written in Tigrinya script a bit like Arabic) and we settled on 'frittata' a sort of scrambled egg with tomato and chili peppers served piping hot in the pan in which it had been cooked. With it we had bread rolls which showed the Italian influence but the tea was Eritrean, served without milk in a small tumbler and was spiced with cinnamon and sugar. We all had the same each with two cups of tea and we were amazed at the bill - 9 Birr 50 cents or just under £1, and this was city prices! This was our first taste of Eritrean food but we were soon to discover how untypical this food was and just how different life was once you left the city.

By mid-afternoon we were beginning to feel the effects of lack of sleep and decided to have a siesta. This set us up for the evening for Duncan had planned to take us out to a restaurant for our first taste of real Eritrean food. The restaurant he chose was very crowded and we had to wait before we were able to get a table, which we took as being a very good sign. We felt that we could have been anywhere in the world until we started to consider what we were to eat. Food in Eritrea is eaten communally, on a single large plate which is approximately 20 inches in diameter. This is placed on a large round pancake called injera which covers the plate. I say pancake because that is the nearest thing we have to it, but it is very unlike anything we know as it is made from Tef, a grain that is unique to Eritrea and Ethiopia. It is dark grey in colour and covered in tiny holes as it is made from a fermented mixture. Depending on the number of people who are eating, additional injeras are folded and laid on the plate, usually directly in front of the diner. On top of these are ladled a variety of meat stews or zigny which are normally highly spiced with a form of dried chilli called berbera. The meat can be beef, lamb, chicken or goat meat or maybe more than one of these. Vegetarian tastes are catered for with portions of mixed potato and carrots, pureed chickpea, spinach and lentils but these last are normally consumed on so-called "fasting days" which occur twice a week for Eritreans. Eating proceeds by tearing a small portion of injera from the edge and, with the right hand only (the left hand is deemed unclean), skilfully wrapping a portion of meat or vegetable in the injera and then placing this in the mouth. We found this a tricky occupation at first to eat without being messy, but with practice we improved. We knew that at some stage we would be eating like this as guests in the houses of some of Duncan's friends so we practised diligently. As this was our first meal we decided to have "a little of everything" as our friendly waiter suggested and we found it both tasty and filling. Again we were the only white faces in the restaurant and it was with great pleasure that the waiters served our meal. Had we chosen an Italian style dish with a knife and fork, as might have been expected, their pleasure would have been diminished

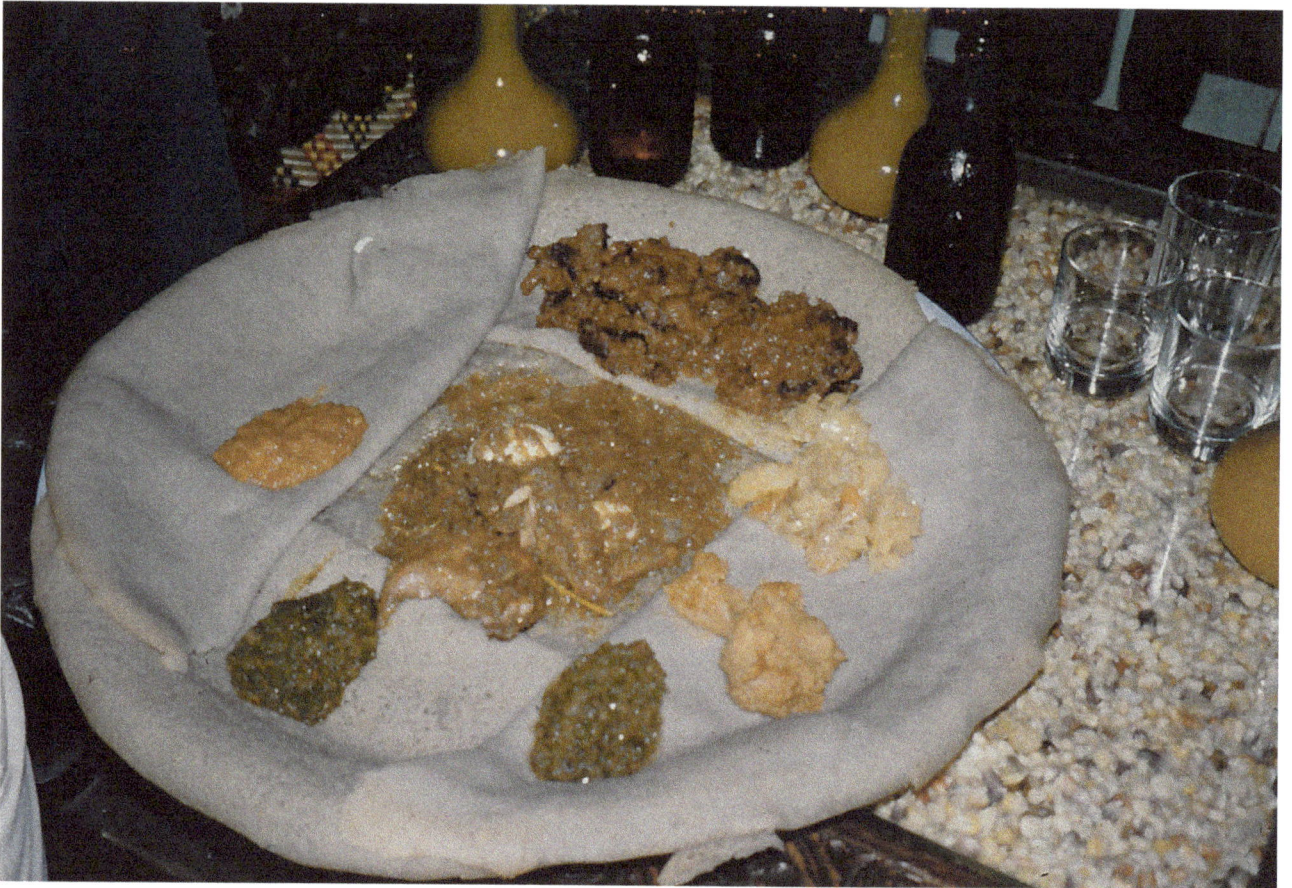

Our first taste of injera with various zignies and vegetable purees

We had received warnings about eating and drinking in Africa but we had already decided that in order that we should not risk offending any host our only concession to "Western standards" would be concerning water. Other than tea or coffee, which is boiled, we only drank bottled beer, mineral water or soft drinks throughout our stay and it was a policy which paid off since neither Jan nor I had a moment's illness during the whole of our stay. We were relieved to find that bottled drinks were available virtually everywhere and were not expensive.

We returned to our hotel walking along busy, lamp-lit roads and our only apprehension was to avoid stepping in the rain-filled potholes. It was very noticeable how unthreatening the people and the general atmosphere was and contrasted favourably with some cities we had visited in both Britain and Europe. We then ended our day with a treat for Duncan. Before we left England he had written to say he would like a taste of the things he missed most and this we had duly provided - Camembert and Cheddar cheese with wholemeal bread and a red wine. This rounded off a memorable day.

We spent just one more day in Asmara, seeing some of the sights and sampling more food. We met seemingly countless people whom Duncan knew, both Eritrean and British, and just progressing along the street involved many stops for conversation. It is one of the charms of the Eritreans that when they meet friends or acquaintances they just will not say hello and pass on, they greet everybody so enthusiastically and warmly that you cannot but respond in like manner and everyone seems the better for it - I think we could learn a lot from this. When a group of people meets another group the minimum that occurs is that everyone shakes hands with each other but, depending on relationships, there are lots of hugging and kissing with everybody laughing and chatting. Men have a special way of greeting other men called bumping. I was introduced to this in somewhat of a hurry when Duncan saw a good friend coming towards us in the main street, Liberation Avenue. He said "Dad I forgot to tell you about bumping, it's going to happen now so just watch and follow what I do". With that he greeted his exuberant friend by shaking hands then with hands still clasped each leant forward and literally bumped shoulders, four or five times and I then followed suit! The conversation at such meetings seemed to follow a pattern for it was customary to introduce those who did not know each other, ask after one's health (and really mean it) and that of one's family, where one had been, and to visitors - did we like Eritrea, Asmara or any other place where we might be? Sometimes the conversation was in English but frequently in Tigrinya and Duncan translated for us. We soon learned that although we could not understand the words we often knew what was being said by the facial expressions and gestures and translation was unnecessary. These conversations were to us a novelty and very interesting, but one could not but contrast such behaviour with our own society where everyone is always in a hurry and we frequently give too little time to our personal relationships.

The next day was time to do some travelling and we split up early to do what was necessary, Duncan to try to hire a car (no advance bookings were accepted) and we to purchase air tickets from Ethiopian Airlines for our planned trip to Ethiopia two weeks later. Duncan had previously told us that he had a longing to go there and we could easily make the journey. We met up later for breakfast, we having been successful but Duncan had not. It seems that when hiring cars one is not asked when it is to be returned so they have no way of knowing when a car would be available. After breakfast Duncan returned again and had more luck and we were shortly able to set off on the first leg of our tour of Eritrea starting with a visit to his village - Tera Emni.

Although the altitude of Tera Emni is above 7000 feet we actually descended from the height of Asmara and our journey south was along twisting roads through the mountains but was mostly downhill. It was not an easy ride because we had a torrential downpour on the way (in the rainy season it seems to rain mostly in the afternoons but this was earlier). However it was dry again as we arrived in Tera Emni and parked the car off the road but some way from Duncan's house. Before we could get out of the car we were surrounded by a crowd of very excited children calling Duncan's name and even he was surprised at the warmth of the welcome and he returned their greetings in their own language. He had been away from the village for several weeks working in Asmara so it was a home-coming welcome for him. We had a lot of luggage in the boot but we were not allowed to carry any of it as a crocodile of children followed Duncan up the rocky path to his house with every item on their heads.

His house was a single storey block built house with a corrugated iron roof but the entrance was walled off with a six foot dry stone wall with a rickety wooden door which created the tiniest of front gardens but at least afforded a little privacy. The children crowded into his house and chatted for a while before slowly drifting away, but no sooner had they gone (presumably to spread the news) than Duncan's friends and neighbours came to see him. Each one came and went individually but for the next hour there were never less than 6 or 7 in the room and of course we had to be introduced and we answered the usual questions. Duncan's next door neighbour, Abrahet, a very excitable and sprightly woman of 65 came in with a basket of freshly cooked injera for us, which must have been quite an expense for her. It is normal on receipt of such a gift to protest and say that one cannot possible accept it but this is always met with a sort of feigned anger until the gift is finally and graciously accepted. This ritual was seen on a number of occasions and as everything is being said in a foreign language one might have assumed that they were having a row, but it always ends in smiles.

All the visitors were asked to return again at 7.30pm for coffee. This might sound a casual invitation but in Eritrea the coffee ceremony is something of a performance akin to the Japanese tea ceremony. The act of making coffee is an art which young women are expected to learn as a basic skill, and takes about an hour to complete. A young teacher colleague of Duncan's, Elsa, took charge of this, and the first thing that is done is to light a small charcoal stove and roast raw coffee beans in a small pan on it until they begin to give off smoke. At this point the pan is taken round the room to each person individually to smell the superb aroma. If the coffee maker is not to be offended each one must express pleasure at this and say "T'oom", which means "delicious". We were not at a loss here for by this time Jan and I were beginning to use some basic Tigrinya expressions which Duncan had taught us in his letters home and we were surprised at their obvious pleasure that we could communicate in their language, even if only in small ways. The roasted coffee beans are then ground by hand using a pestle and mortar, then put into a round-based clay coffee pot with water and brought to the boil on the charcoal. Since the single opening at the top is small and the clay pot is non-transparent, it is necessary to keep a close watch on it lest it boil over. When the coffee is ready the coffee pot is plugged with a horse-hair filter and the coffee poured into small glass tumblers with a large amount of sugar. It is very strong, sweet and delicious. Later more water is added to the coffee pot and subsequent drinks are slightly weaker. Whilst this was happening the party was lively and we got to know each other better. We already knew a lot about Duncan's friends and colleagues (and they us) through Duncan, and we came to learn just how well Duncan was respected for the efforts he had made in adapting to Eritrean customs and food and his facility in their language Tigrinya. We all sat round the room lit by a solitary oil lamp (there is no electricity in Tera

Emni) and drank coffee, ate freshly cooked salted pop-corn, roasted corn cobs and biscuits. After the third cup of coffee had been drunk it is the custom for visitors to leave and so ended our first day. We pulled out our mattresses loaned from VSO and slept like tops.

The next day we found we had to revise our intended plans for the rest of our stay. We wanted to tour Eritrea and we had booked a week in Ethiopia a country which Duncan had never seen, and this would take up the balance of our planned three weeks. But we had also received many invitations to visit the homes of Duncan's friends and there was just insufficient time to do it all. Since we felt we could not be selective over these visits (we would only offend those omitted) we had no choice but to consider staying longer, but as this would involve changing our air-tickets we decided to leave it to Ethiopian Airways and fate. Our journey involved returning via Asmara so we would go to the airline office to try to extend our stay and go back to England a little later.

Duncan was still on summer holiday from school and we had planned to stay only one night in Terra Emni as we were about to tour Eritrea and Ethiopia. We intended to come back for a couple of days especially to see Duncan's class when the school resumed but as these invitations were difficult to refuse we said that we would return after our tour and hoped that we could change our flight home to extend our stay.

We woke the following morning in Duncan's house to a wild cacophony consisting of cockerels crowing, dogs barking, donkeys braying, and a noise from the roof which sounded like someone with hob-nailed boots clumping up and down. It turned out to be nothing more than a flock of pigeons but on the corrugated iron roof it seemed to amplify the sound. This apparently is normal but we were experiencing what every day life was like for Duncan. Our first requirement was to go outside to a nearby field of maize as there is no form of sanitation in the village. On return, our ablutions were done with a minimum amount of water in a small bowl as water is a problem in the village. About half a mile away is a well but the pump which had been installed was broken and as the sides of the well were steep it was difficult to get water in much quantity. However as it was the rainy season Duncan had a full barrel of rainwater which we used, but as we were now three instead of one, we knew it had to be used, sparingly. We used a small amount of Duncan's drinking water to brush our teeth. Drinking water is obtained by boiling the well water and then putting it into a filter which looks like a small tea urn (this had been provided by VSO and was the extent of Duncan's modern equipment).

We breakfasted on rolls and cheese which we had brought with us and tea made Eritreans style, that is coriander spiced and drunk without milk. Afterwards we re-packed for our journey. This was necessary because we intended to leave behind our heavy suitcases which contained a large amount of presents which we knew would be required for our visiting and also books which we had brought from England to give to Tera Emni School. We needed to travel light and we had brought haversacks for this purpose.

Our hired car was parked on a flat piece of ground near the road and as we carried our bags towards it we were again assisted by the children. As we had to walk through part of the village we inevitably met and were greeted by some of Duncan's friends who by now we regarded as our friends also despite the short time of our acquaintance. Each greeting was so enthusiastic that we set off flushed with pleasure at starting the morning so well.

It was a bright sunny morning as we set off south towards our first stop, Mendafera, the regional capital. We passed through a few small villages on the way, and all around were fields rich in agriculture. But here people had to live on what they grew so we saw many people working in the fields. This was the rainy season but I knew that it was to be followed by a six or more months without rain so I asked Duncan how they managed to irrigate their fields during that period. In answer he took a side turning, no more than a stony track, to a recently built earth dam, behind which a lake was developing. This would eventually control water supply to the fields during the dry season when the river virtually dried up.

We continued on towards Mendefera through similar agricultural land and when we arrived at the start of the town we saw what looked like a road block that is a rope stretched across the road with nearby a small hut around which stood officials. As we approached the rope was lowered and Duncan tooted his horn in appreciation. This is the Eritrean equivalent of the local customs officers which we saw as we came into every large town. They can stop any vehicle and search it but in practice only stop lorries. They are there to ensure that appropriate customs duties are paid and to stop illegal carriage of goods. Any duties raised go to the local community.

As we entered the town I thought it was more like a large village. Despite its importance this town was very unprepossessing and very unlike Asmara. The buildings were low single story block built dwellings frequently consisting of single rooms with window spaces without glass, covered at night with metal shutters. There were signs of newer bigger buildings being constructed but there was no real style, no Italian influence, except maybe for St George's Church on the hill. Side roads were almost all muddy tracks except in the town centre where we stopped to explore. After a short stop for drinks on the shady terrace of a restaurant (we all drank the local bottled effervescent mineral water), Duncan took us to the market where we needed to make some purchases. The market was large and sprawling and I soon realised why this town was important. It may have started as a market town, but now being on the main road from Asmara to Ethiopia in the south, it was the centre of local industry. Here we saw not only traders but the artisans too. There were metal workers with their cutters and hammers and a huge pile of cans of various sizes which was their raw material. Tailors were hard at work with treadle-operated sewing machines making colourful dresses and shirts; simple rustic furniture was being made consisting of a wooden frame with stretched goat hide for seats (it was here that Duncan must have purchased his sofa). The main market area had regular traders in somewhat battered stalls with rusty corrugated roofs and plastic sheets to keep out the rain, but on the periphery and in the side streets sat women with their few home-grown wares laid out on the ground hoping to make a sale. Duncan made for the stalls where he knew from experience the best produce was sold at reasonable prices (bargaining is the norm here and you pay whatever you can). It should not have surprised us, but it did, that he and we were greeted like long lost friends. We purchased some fruit but before we left we were offered a gift of a guava each specially selected for its ripeness. This gave us a few qualms because guava can be eaten like an apple and it was clear that we were intended to both eat and appreciate them in front of the donor. We had a health rule that said only eat peeled fruit and I did not at that time have my pen knife with me. We nevertheless ate and thoroughly enjoyed both them and the obvious pleasure he got from our acceptance. Eritreans just love to give presents and I suppose, like us all, want to have them appreciated. Fortunately we had no ill effects from this but I endeavoured always to carry my pen knife in my pocket after that.

Duncan also needed to purchase wood for his Mogogo (a wood burning stove for making injera which he intended to have a try at). This was no casual purchase because I was amazed at the actual weight of each piece which is dense hardwood heavier than oak. He had planned to use the boot of the car to get a reasonable load; otherwise he would have had to make many trips by bicycle to get as much. We had seen wood being carried along that road on people's heads, mostly women, and now I appreciated the weight I had renewed respect for their efforts. We needed a receipt to prove that he had purchased it legally because wood is a precious commodity and is controlled in Eritrea since the war, there being little natural woodland left in the country. This is because it had been largely felled during the long drawn out war, and only since the war ended had any attempts been made at reforestation and this would take many years. Duncan's receipt would be needed as we left town.

We had noticed on both sides of the highway at about 100 yard intervals were wigwams of metal within which grew a young sapling tree. We discovered that these extended the length and breadth of the country on every main highway and had been planted as a living memorial to those who had died in "the struggle" as the war is described. The survival of every tree is the responsibility of each community, the watering of which is no easy task in the dry season. These trees replace the thousands of trees which were destroyed during the struggle. It is an outward sign of the strong sense of nationhood that exists in Eritrea and demonstrates how hard everyone is working to literally rebuild the country.

After we had sheltered from the torrential rain which appeared on cue in the early afternoon, we turned north again towards Asmara, our next destination, stopping in Tera Emni long enough to unload the wood, again assisted by the ever-present children. In Asmara we returned to the same hotel in the evening and we were pleased that we were allocated the same rooms as on our first stay.

The next day we went out for breakfast as previously and on returning to the hotel to book out, Duncan bumped into two VSO colleagues in the street. They were returning to their posts in Agordat in the north-west having spent a short holiday in Ethiopia. We offered them a lift in the car as we were about to go to Keren which although it is due north from Asmara was on the only road to Agordat and was about half way for them. We were pleased to have their company but it wasn't easy getting all the extra luggage we had between us into the boot and it was somewhat cramped. The journey to Keren is about 60 miles but we anticipated a journey of between 2 and 3 hours because the road is through very mountainous country on roads that were good in places where recent renovation had taken place and not quite so good in others. On the journey we learned that Mark is a maths teacher and Andy teaches agricultural methodology and we discovered that because Agordat is in the lowlands, it is hot and dusty for much of the year and is difficult to reach except in a four-wheeled-drive vehicle due to the state of the roads.

The journey north was through spectacular landscape and was much greener than we had expected. Where the land was flatter and on the lower slopes agriculture is again very much in evidence with maize, wheat and Tef (the grain used for injera) being most predominant, but a variety of vegetables were also being grown. Again there was no sign of any form of agricultural machinery and manual labour was mostly the norm except where bullocks were used for ploughing and donkeys or mules for carrying. We passed through no more than three villages on the way and in each were domestic animals, attended by little boys aged between 6 and 8 who knew how to handle their herds of cattle, sheep or goats. We could only marvel at the skill of these young children.

Keren is set on a high plateau some 5000 feet above sea level but we were actually descending to it as Asmara is some 2500 feet higher. At this lower level the temperature is warmer and very pleasant. The town was bathed in sunshine as we approached and this was reflected from the white buildings which predominated. This town looks and feels very Moslem with the muezzin towers of the various mosques dominating the skyline. We found our hotel which was a single story building with all the rooms looking out onto a beautiful courtyard which was shaded by a canopy of vines. The room was clean but rather basic with a bed, a rather battered wardrobe and a table being the only furniture. There was a washbasin with taps but all the plumbing had been removed! Next to this was a large bucket full of clean water and under the sink was a bowl to catch the outflow. We laughed at the surprise and laughed still more when we tried to turn on the light in the rather dark room but there was no electricity. Duncan later explained that they only have electricity in the hotel from dusk to midnight.

We explored the town and especially the market which was much poorer but more exotic than those in Asmara or Mendafera. There were animals everywhere, especially camels and every other person wore seemingly spotless white robes. The smell of large mounds of spices also gave the air a pungent aroma. This had once been an Italian town and we found a wide variety of housing from the very grand to the ramshackle. In particular the former railway station (the rail track had long since been removed) looked as if it had seen better days and was now a very run-down hotel.

Just a little outside the town Jan and I went to see the British Cemetery. This was in a walled garden, immaculately maintained in direct contrast to the dry scrub land which surrounded it. (The British War Graves Commission pays for its upkeep) We could not initially get in as the gate was locked, but I climbed over the wall and was shortly joined by a man who appeared from nowhere who turned out to be the custodian who then let my wife in. We examined the lines of headstones which told their own grim story of young men who had been killed in Eritrea in World War II. We found it very sad that it was apparent from the wording on them that many of these graves had been unvisited by their families. We were then shown a visitors book which contained a short history of the battle for Keren in 1941. It soon became apparent that the cemetery was established close to the scene of the battle between the British and Italians, and the hill which overlooked us was named 'Cameron's Ridge". It was not difficult to imagine that battle scene and we found this sudden realisation very moving and we left the cemetery with lumps in our throats.

The next day we returned to Asmara to start the next leg of our journey by flying to Ethiopia.

Every road in Eritrea whether to North South East or West leads you back to the capital Asmara, and we returned there to start the next leg of our tour by flying to Ethiopia. Before we did this however we had another important job to do, to visit Ethiopian Airways to try to extend our stay. The airline office was in the centre of town, in Liberation Avenue and we were somewhat dismayed to find the office apparently shut with a metal roll-up security gate halfway closed. On closer inspection we found that this was only a measure to prevent the interior from being overcrowded and we shortly were allowed in, were allocated a number and awaited our turn. It took more than an hour to be seen but we were very impressed with the calm methodical approach taken by the assistant and also were relieved to realise that she spoke excellent English and had access to modern computers for booking purposes. Yes, we could not only change our tickets but had a choice of five different days to return. We extended by a full week, picked up our new tickets and left. We had a few qualms about whether we had any appointments in England in that week (we just could not remember) and we needed to let our family know of the changed flight details, so our next port of call was to the Asmara VSO office. We knew they had a fax machine and we were able to send a fax to our eldest son Graham at his office. We need not have worried for within 15 minutes we had a reply which confirmed that he would make any re-arrangements necessary for us. We could now go off to Ethiopia in good heart.

ETHIOPIA

The early flight to Addis Ababa took only a little over an hour and it was still early when we got there. We circled the city before landing and we could see that it was very large and sprawled haphazardly between the surrounding hills. Its population is about 1.5 million and at 7,500 feet above sea level it is the third highest capital in the world.

Our first action was to seek a telephone to book a hotel taken from our guide book which was done quite easily. We then got into a rather battered blue taxi to take us to the hotel, having first bartered the cost and paying half the originally stated price. The hotel was some three miles from the centre and on one of the main roads leading into the city. The hotel was quite new and very comfortable but having settled in briefly we were off again, this time to book flights to the towns of Bahar Dar and Lalibela which we wanted to visit. Yet another run-down taxi took us to the centre of Addis. It was a straight drive along a dual carriageway into the centre but progress was slow due partly to the terrible state of the roads which were full of potholes and partly the age of the taxi. Strangely it was also due to the fact that there were frequently goats, cattle or donkeys being herded along the main road. In a modern city it looked most incongruous, but later as we neared the centre, at each traffic light that our taxi stopped we were surrounded by beggars, many of them children, putting their hands in through the windows seeking money. This was our first taste of such aggressive begging as there had been virtually none in Eritrea but we were to see much more of this in Addis. We bought our flight tickets very easily but found we had to leave the very next day, so despite our tiredness we decided to explore the city straight away.

Addis Ababa has many high rise modern buildings in the centre but in the suburbs most buildings were low and often in a poor state of repair. We could not but contrast this with Asmara which was much cleaner and compact. There was also a very different feel to this city, for as we walked around we were approached continually by beggars or street vendors pressing their wares. On one occasion Duncan was offered a newspaper which was thrust at him, but this was only a decoy and he immediately felt the vendor trying to pick his shirt pocket and angrily pushed him away. This put us on our guard, but we later noticed that this aggression appeared to be confined to the centre of the city and we met no problems elsewhere. We bought a meal in a quiet restaurant set back from the noise of the road and made our plans. We decided to do some shopping because we had seen some handicraft items for sale which interested us, but then to return to our hotel for the night. Staying in Addis after dark did not appeal to us so we were glad to return to the comfort of our hotel.

The next day we returned to Addis Ababa airport for our flight to Bahar Dar but after the usual formalities we were to encounter a degree of security which we had so far not met. All passengers had to undergo a body search and hand luggage was examined thoroughly. I had in my pocket a small penknife and when this was discovered I thought at first it was going to be confiscated but when I protested I was assured in sign language (for there was no English spoken here) that it would be placed in a box with other similar items from other passengers and returned to me after the flight. An airport bus took us across the airfield to our plane but before we could board we found that a second body search was necessary. At the time this seemed somewhat excessive and irritating but it was less than two months later that an Ethiopian Airlines jet was hi-jacked from this very airport and later crashed into the sea off the East African coast. In retrospect we realised that the security was necessary for our own protection. The flight north took just 35 minutes and by lunch time we had arrived in the small town of Bahar Dar on the southern bank of the enormous Lake Tana. At its widest points this lake is more than 30 miles wide from North to South and a similar distance from East to West, making it more like an inland sea. It is in fact the source of the Blue Nile River and was one of our reasons for coming here. We were taken to our lakeside hotel by mini-bus (reasonably good compared to the Addis transportation) and once again settled in. The gardens of this hotel are rightly famed for their beauty with flowers of all colours in bloom and many trees ripe with fruit. I recognised mangos and figs but could not name the others. The trees were filled with birds, many with bright red or yellow plumage again I could not name them, it was a riot of colour.

Later we walked about a mile or so down the road to a bridge across the Blue Nile itself. It was not blue however, being a rather muddy yellow colour due to this being the rainy season. The ground itself was very muddy which gave every sign of the amount of local rain but so far we had seen no rain. We came to the river because we had been told that one might see both crocodiles and hippos there but we didn't see them either. We were approached on this walk by a young boy called Davit who said in very good English that he could arrange transport for us to see the Tississat Falls. This was the main tourist attraction in the area so it was no surprise that this offer was made to us. His price for a 4 wheel drive vehicle (a must on the muddy tracks we were to drive on) was cheaper than those we had seen on offer at our hotel so we agreed. Later we met a Dutch lady, Sascha, and a French soldier, Jerome, whom we had first spoken to on the plane and they asked to be included on the trip for a share of the cost. We were happy to have their company and we agreed to pick them up at their hotel at 6.30 the next morning.

It was still dark when we arose the next morning to go to breakfast and sure enough there was our young friend Davit standing with two adults by a land cruiser waiting for us outside the hotel. They were early and we were hungry but we made a quick meal before setting off for the falls, picking up our friends on the way, at which point Davit and one of the men left us with just the driver. It is some 30 miles to the Tisabay village which was our destination and once outside of the town the road degenerated to a stony track which in places was very muddy. It was a very bumpy ride but as the sun came up we realised that we were going to have a warm sunny day which would be good for photography. This was arable country which we were passing through and the green lush fields we saw were in some places flooded. Tisabay village is very poor, but it occurred to us that if the tourist industry ever took off in Ethiopia this might change. The housing was totally made of tree branches and thatch; people were dressed very poorly, frequently barefooted and some of the children especially did not look well. Many of the children wanted to assist us on our way to the falls which were still some 40 minutes walk away over very rugged terrain and the five of us were surrounded by a posse of them as we slowly made our way over the hill. One little bare-foot girl of about 8 or 9 attached herself to my wife

Jan to show her the best paths to take and she, being more sure-footed than any of us, was a great help to her.

We could hear the roar of the falls well before they came into view and we were not disappointed. What a magnificent sight they were, some quarter of a mile wide and falling perhaps 200 or 300 feet. The volume of water that cascades here, especially as it was the rainy season, was immense and we just stood in awe. There is a permanent rainbow over the falls caused by the spray and it was ideal light for photography. We stayed quite some time both for photographs and to rest but as we returned we were surrounded by the children who now wanted us to buy their brightly coloured pots made from gourds which they had been carrying. We bartered for them as is the custom but the prices we settled at were not high but were highly valued by them. Later we stopped for refreshments which we had not eaten on the plane but carried with us. We found that we could not eat in front of the children and we gave our limited snacks to them wishing it were more. A girl who was slightly older than the rest unwrapped a slice of cake, divided it up, and then shared it with the others. She then took the cling film and carefully smoothed it so that it could be used again. In this country nothing is wasted.

We were pleased to return to the village and our transport which was again surrounded by more children. We tried to talk to them but none knew more than a few words of English, but several gave us pieces of paper with their names and addresses carefully written on them (probably by someone else) and asked us to send them clothes. It was a heart-rending experience.

When we returned to Bahar Dar we made some enquiries about hiring a boat to go out on the lake but were told that all boats had been requisitioned to aid in flood relief around the lake, which at this point we were unaware of. We looked round the town for a while and although there seemed some small degree of prosperity in places, there was also a great deal of poverty. Some people were living in temporary shelters of tree branches and thatch by the side of the road and many looked very ill.

It all contrasted greatly with the hotel area where we were staying and left us all with a guilt complex when we compared ourselves with them. This must be a typical feeling for tourists in third world countries but there seems so little that one can do except at the individual level. Later in the afternoon it started to rain and we were soon to realise just how fortunate we had been with the weather on our trip to Tississat for it became torrential and lasted the rest of the day and most of the night.

We had a morning flight for the next leg of our triangular tour of Ethiopia and so we got out our waterproof coats and huddled into the minibus to the airfield. When we got there the weather was bad enough to cause concern that our flight might not arrive and we were delayed for over an hour. There was no staff at the airfield so we had no communication. There were very few people waiting except those who intended to fly to Lalibela, our next stop, and we used this time to get to know some of our travelling companions. We were to become a happy group of nine "Europeans" over the next few days and we did virtually everything together whilst our travels coincided.

The light aircraft eventually came and we took off quickly and flew low enough to be under the thick cloud above us. As we flew round the lake edge we could see the flooding below us and only then realised the extent of the problem. Bahar Dar had been muddy but must have been high enough not to be affected by flooding and we had escaped the problem. Soon we had left the area of the lake and suddenly we emerged into brilliant sunshine and could see a magnificent landscape below us. Flying low we were able to see the countryside so clearly that it took ones breath away. There was so much green everywhere and the steep chasms and valleys with meandering rivers were spectacular but must make travelling on land very difficult. We saw only occasional habitation, small groups of houses that were too small to be villages indicated that these were for the people who worked on the land and there were signs of extensive agriculture.

We landed on a rough airstrip in a field and were met by an open backed truck to transport us with our baggage to Lalibela which was still 40 minutes drive away over incredibly rocky and hilly but spectacular country. We were not surprised to learn later that during the wet season Lalibela is accessible only by air. We were here primarily to see the incredible rock-hewn churches which had been literally carved down into the rock in the twelfth century which were said to contain the original Arc of the Covenant, but after we had spent our allotted two days here we virtually all agreed that this had been the best part of our journey.

On arrival we knew that we had to hire a reliable English speaking guide to take us over the twelve churches, and we were lucky to get a man who spoke excellent English and was not only knowledgeable about the history of the churches but helpful in a variety of other ways. Our tour began that very afternoon and we were soon introduced into their mysteries.

Getting a panoramic photograph of many of them was very difficult because by their very nature they were all sunk below ground level in what was effectively a 50ft pit with sheer walls close to the walls of the churches. It seemed incredible that what we saw had not been built up but carved down in the rock for they were as ornate as any church to be seen elsewhere with elaborate carvings and windows. The churches are not museums but living churches with services held every day. Each one has its own priest who is dressed in highly ornate and colourful robes and carrying gilded crosses. Every one of these priests was prepared to pose in front of their drapes and tapestries for the tourist's cameras provided they were not due to officiate at a service at which visitors were frequently excluded. What also amazed us was that we were allowed to examine and turn the pages of bibles made of goat-skin which were hand-written in the twelfth century. When I commented on this it was met with a shrug of the shoulders.

Inside each church was inevitably dark despite the windows, but when one got used to the gloom one could see delicately carved archways and statues, altars covered in brightly coloured drapes and ancient paintings on goatskin. It is claimed that the Ark of the Covenant is held here but only the appointed guardian priest is allowed to see it.

Lalibela Priest

After we had made our way through about half of the churches we returned to our hotel to rest, but not before we had arranged that next day we would have an early morning mule trek to what was called a cave church, followed by the continuation of our tour in the afternoon.

Later in the day we were walking through the village when we came upon a young bare-foot boy of about 5 or 6 who had badly gashed his toe and was crying pitifully. He had a deep wound which needed cleaning and as it seemed that no-one was going to give him any appropriate help we told an older boy who was with him that we would help. Jan tried to calm him down whilst I ran back to our hotel and got our first-aid box and a bottle of water. When I returned we had been joined by an adult villager who said he had medical knowledge and so we made our limited facilities available to him. What followed I found disturbing because we had gathered a crowd of villagers around us and several of them asked for medical attention assuming we were doctors or nurses. We were able to give out some first aid dressings but were unable to assist others whom we assumed were ill. We left our first aid box with the man to use the best he could. Later we were told that there was indeed a clinic in the village but we never learned whether the facilities there were free or not because it was clear that most would have been unable to pay.

Later that evening all the Europeans ate together in the hotel and we chatted excitedly about our day. In discussion one person expressed regret that there was not a common language for all people to communicate with each other, but he seemed to miss the point that we were all speaking English both to each other and throughout Ethiopia. We could only smile at this but we felt it unfair to point it out.

One of our group, Pepe, was late for dinner and when he arrived he was looking very pale. When we asked him what was his problem he said he had been bitten on the toe by a scorpion whilst taking a shower, and he was in some discomfort. When doubt was expressed about whether it was indeed a scorpion he returned to his room and produced the dead creature and it was, though it seemed small, about the size of a large spider. We were all worried for no-one knew how serious it was, and there was no medical help available at that time, and we were not helped by the hotelier's views that we should cut round the wound. One of our group was in fact a nurse and she applied a tourniquet for a short while, and cleaned the toe and waited to see what developed. In fact nothing did happen although Pepe's evening was spoiled. Fortunately he had recovered somewhat by the next day. It was our second time within a few hours that we had cause to be concerned over medical aid, or its lack.

We had a very early start the next morning and darkness was just lifting as we set out on mule-back to the cave church. Jan and I had never ridden in our lives but we were pleased that we proceeded at no more than a fast walking pace with a young boy literally trotting alongside holding the rein. The terrain we crossed was very rugged and rock-strewn but largely uphill on the outward journey. To our surprise we quickly got used to the ride and as the sun came up we were lost in wonder at the beautiful scenery we passed by. Everything was so green and on such a large scale with deep ravines and steep cliff faces in all directions. It took an hour and a half to reach our destination and we rested the mules but we were glad to rest too (I hadn't realised how tiring riding could be). The young boys had been magnificent and did not seem tired and I suspected that we may have been accompanied by some future Olympic Champion long distance runner that the Ethiopians seem continually to produce.

The church was in effect an ornately built wall which covered the front of a large overhang of rock which became the roof, but the wall did not quite reach the roof. We had to wait outside the church for a service to end before we could enter and were surprised at the depth of the church. In the first chamber were sculptured rocks with pools of water catching drips permeating through the rock of the roof, which having been blessed by the priest became holy water. We were permitted to drink this spring water and this was the only time we had other than bottled water in our entire journey. Once again we were shown the church finery and relics by the priest and spent about half an hour there.

Our return was just as splendid as the outward journey but this time we found that we were progressively joined by people making their way to Lalibela market. The nearer we got to the town the more people there were and could be counted in their hundreds. Most people were carrying goods to sell or herding livestock but all were walking and some would have walked many miles. What we found particularly fascinating was that apart from ourselves and our fellow tourists everyone was dressed much as they would have been in biblical times, nor could we see any tools or implements which betrayed that we were in fact in the 20th Century except for the occasional plastic containers for liquids. Jan said that the effect of this and the huge numbers made her feel that we were in a gigantic Cecil B DeMille film production.

We could not resist going to the market as soon as we had returned and parted with the mules. This was easier said than done because there were literally thousands cramming into the narrow thoroughfares before we were able to see from a hill just how packed the market area was. We slowly made our way round but it was hard at times to make any progress in the throng largely because many people came as sellers as well as buyers. Despite the apparent chaos we could see that there were defined areas for each type of produce and people had laid their wares out mostly on cloths or plastic sheets on the ground, and then sat beside them waiting for customers. There was no overt selling and they mostly sat patiently waiting for customers. Fresh food and household items such as pots and pans made up the majority, but there was one man whose activity intrigued us. He was sitting crossed-legged and cutting a large block of greyish-white stone-with a saw. It took great effort and he reduced the block to smaller brick sized lumps. I could not guess what it was, and not until we returned to our hotel and found someone who spoke English did I discover that it was nothing more than a block of salt.

One field adjacent to the market was set aside for live animals and we made our way there to see it. As we wandered through the crowd there was a sudden shout and people were running in all directions which opened up a space before me just as I saw a large black bull rush past. A black woman shouted in English "Is there no woman here who can control this cow?" This comment somehow seemed to relieve the tension and everyone, ourselves included, burst into laughter. It was caught soon after. We were reluctant to leave the market but we still had further churches to visit so we made our way slowly up the hill to the hotel.

A crowded Lalibela Market

After lunch our guide led us to those churches which were furthest away and it seemed we were shown those with the most climbing down up or through. There were innumerable underground passages connecting them. We finished our tour by wondering why these churches had not been designated The Eighth Wonder of the Ancient World.

We were all extremely tired after our various excursions and we all decided on an early night as we were due to fly back to Addis Ababa the next day. Without exception this part of our trip had been the most memorable and even now I can see the sights of Lalibela in my mind's eye more clearly than any other.

The next day we were taken on the "joy ride" as we referred to the incredibly bumpy journey to the airfield. Despite the fact that there was no building on this field other than an old wooden barn, we went through the now familiar security procedures before boarding the light aircraft to Addis. In little more than an hour we had arrived and it was interesting how the contrast with the primitive conditions of both Bahar Dar and Lalibela made this city now seem more modern than before, despite the decrepit taxis we had to use. I have made several references to this but we had more taxi experiences to come.

We stayed in Addis for two more nights, giving us a full day for shopping for presents to take home and doing some sight-seeing. At one point we went into the main Post Office to send off some letters and cards but before we could enter we were again body-searched. This is the security procedure for all Government Buildings and the Post Office was no exception.

Later we decided to walk to the Museum which was some way from the centre but the map we were using was somewhat misleading and we seriously under-estimated the distance. It was now early afternoon and we could see dark thunderclouds forming so we decided to go into a nearby restaurant for lunch, hoping the rain would have passed when we were finished. However it had not, and when we came to leave the rain was still torrential. We also did not know how far we had to travel so decided to call a taxi. This was difficult as every one which passed was full. At this point a little boy came up to us and said he would get us a taxi if we waited and off he went in the rain. Some five minutes later he was as good as his word when he arrived in the taxi itself and we all got in. I naturally tipped the boy for his trouble but was surprised to see the taxi driver do the same. We bargained for the fare to the museum agreed a price and then settled back as the taxi went off. But soon we realised that the taxi driver did not know where it was. He continually turned corners and we were sure on one occasion that we had been along the same street earlier. Eventually he stopped and went over to a taxi-driver colleague to ask the way. It was still some distance but we got there having travelled for some 25 minutes on a journey that I estimate should have been less than 10 minutes judging by the fare we had paid. In the process we had now totally lost our sense of direction.

The museum was not large and we had the services of a woman who was very knowledgeable to guide us round. The main item we had come to see was known as "Lucy" which is the name given to the remains of the oldest human (Homo sapiens) yet found - 3.5 million years old and found in central Ethiopia. We stayed about an hour and then decided to leave as I had to get to the Eritrean Embassy to collect our passports with re-entry permits. It had now stopped raining, although everywhere was saturated so we decided to get another taxi. There was no boy available to help this time so we just walked (hopefully in the right direction) seeking the familiar blue colour. When we started looking I had 30 minutes to get to the Embassy, but 20 minutes later we had had no luck, until at last there was one parked in the main road ahead of us. As we approached we could see the driver sitting in his seat apparently asleep, but when we tapped on his window he awoke and seemed anxious for our custom. He got out and we quickly agreed a price for the fare - I was also anxious that he knew where to go but as the Embassy was in Maskell Square, which was almost in the city centre this presented no problem. He had great difficulty in opening the passenger doors for us, and once we were in had further difficultly in closing them. As we sat down we could see just how decrepit this vehicle was, but we had no choice if we were not to be late. The driver got in, turned round and asked if he could have the fare in advance. This was most unusual and when we asked why, he said that he had no petrol and could not start without some. We agreed and he got a petrol can from his boot and ran off down the road at which point we wondered whether he intended returning, but no, he came back and poured the petrol in the tank. He then went to the front and raised the bonnet and we could see him climbing almost into the engine compartment to blow the carburettor in order to get the petrol circulating. This had taken up our entire spare time and I just hoped the journey would be quick, but there was more to come. He inevitably had difficulty starting the engine and we were almost on the point of exasperation when it started. All of us sitting in the taxi in the humid conditions had steamed up all his windows and he could not see ahead. He just gave a huge grin and reached out for his windscreen wiper which was lying loose on the dashboard instead of on the outside. He calmly wiped the inside windows with this and set off, initially doing a U-turn right across the path of on-coming traffic. The ride was appalling and I realised that he had a rear puncture. When I told him this he just laughed and said he knew and drove on. We were all laughing by this time - almost hysterically - and my next fear was for his brakes. We were descending from a steep hill towards the city centre with many sets of traffic lights and it was with amazement and no little relief when he was able to stop at the first red light. However he lost the engine at this point and could not restart. Traffic was honking and going round us but by the time he restarted the lights were red again. This happened twice and I wondered whether we would ever get there, but we did, some 20 minutes late and fortunately this turned out to be no problem. The taxi we had travelled in was nothing more than a death trap yet there were others almost as bad wherever we went.

The next day we flew back to Asmara for our final emotional week.

Return to ERITREA

We flew from Addis Ababa to Asmara on New Year's Eve - that is the Ethiopian Coptic church's New Year. The date was 10th September 1996 in our calendar but we were on the verge of 1989 in their calendar as they are 7 years behind us. Asmara Airport was lightly draped in coloured paper chains by way of celebration and looked quite festive but that was not all, for when we had left only 1 week earlier, the airport was looking like a building site, but now the concrete columns were all marble clad, a modern false ceiling with fluorescent lighting inset now hid what was a mass of cables; new furniture and fittings had been placed in the formerly dilapidated arrivals hall. In short a marvellous transformation had taken place and not for the first time had we wondered at the speed of change that the Eritreans were achieving.

When we had once again booked into what we had started to call "our hotel" in the city centre we went out to see the sights. The streets were crowded and many people were dressed in their "Sunday Best", especially the children, and we exchanged greetings with many passers-by. "Rhus owdie amet" is the equivalent Tigrinya for "Happy New Year" but occasionally we were greeted with "Bona fiesta" from older people who still spoke Italian. We saw some children had lighted faggots of wood which smouldered giving off smoke and they invited people to step over the faggots in one direction and then back again to greet the New Year which was a time-honoured custom. Of course one gave them small change for the favour - much as one might give "a penny for the guy" in England.

At lunchtime the next day Duncan reminded us that we were to take up the first of our invitations. We were to share the equivalent of a Christmas Dinner with the family of Girmai who was the deputy headmaster at Duncan's school in Tera Emni. They lived in a two roomed house in the run-down suburb of Haz Haz on the outskirts of Asmara, but Girmai worked in Tera Emni during the week and returned home only at weekends. Despite his status at school we knew that the family had financial problems largely because he had nine children in all and the eldest, Salamawit, had a baby of her own. Duncan knew the family well for he had been lodging with them earlier in the summer when he was working in Asmara. We caught a bus to Haz Haz and were greeted so enthusiastically by To'erbay, Germai's wife that we felt like old family friends even though we had never met her. Although Girmai speaks excellent English his wife does not, but this seemed to make little difference for even when Duncan did not translate for us we could guess what she was saying. Only the adults sat down to eat in the sparsely furnished main room and we were given a traditional injera meal, but this time it was in Ethiopian style for we ate off separate plates. This was accompanied by Suwa (the unfortunately named home-brewed beer of Eritrea) and Areki, a spirit similar to Pernod. The meal was finished off with coffee traditionally made by Salamawit their daughter. Throughout the meal the children came and went, curious to see the white visitors and giggling when we spoke to them. Although as guests we had brought presents for the family we were surprised and moved when we were presented with a traditional hide covered basket as a parting gift from the family

In the evening we had been invited to have coffee at the house of Elsa's aunt (Elsa was a teaching colleague of Duncan). Elsa normally lived in Tera Emni but was spending her summer holidays in Asmara and it was to here that we were invited, together with Habtom, another of Duncan's teacher colleagues. Again a bus ride was necessary to reach the house and it was getting dark when we arrived. We were greeted by Elsa this time dressed in traditional robes and looking very beautiful. Previously we had seen her dressed in modern western style and always looking smart, but the robes gave her a new sort of elegance. She introduced us to her elderly aunt who was similarly dressed but this was the only time we spoke to her because she retired to another room, apparently she was in mourning for her sister who had recently died. The invitation to "coffee" had been a misnomer because we were treated to a full scale injera meal which was almost the same as we had had at Girmai's house. It was like having two Christmas dinners on one day but we had to do justice to it or else offend our hosts. Elsa's family have European connections and it was apparent by the furnishings that there were few financial problems in this house. There were sofas, armchairs and cupboards and curtaining which we had not seen before in any home. There on the ornate sideboard sitting in pride of place was a TV set, We watched a little of this later in the evening for broadcasting only lasts a few hours a day (much like the early days of BBC) and was a must for those lucky enough to have it. We understand that during the week all the nine languages of Eritrea are represented in broadcasts but on this evening we saw a film of the Independence Day celebrations which was broadcast in Tigrinya so we had some of the commentary translated for us. It was late when we left and had to get a taxi home.

We stayed a further night in Asmara and the next day we went for coffee, as had become our custom, to the restaurant in the centre which was used as the main meeting place by all the VSO. It was very busy as usual, when a large group of young people arrived and Duncan realised that these were the latest VSO volunteer contingent. He went over to introduce himself and welcome the newcomers to Eritrea. We watched the group as he was talking and we noticed one black girl who seemed to stand out from the rest. This may have been because her hair was braided and fell down her back below her waist with a scarf holding it together part way down. It was the longest hair I had ever seen. We realised later how important it was to greet newcomers and help them relax for some may have had apprehensions about their new undertaking.

Later Duncan returned to Tera Emni because he had preparation to do for the new school term and we thought it best if we stayed out of his way for a little. We also had to confirm our return flight home at the end of that week so we again visited Ethiopian Airways office.

Eventually the time came for us to make our way to the bus station to find a bus going to Tera Emni. There were large crowds at the station and we had to ask many tines before we found the right bus. No bus leaves until it is full so we had anticipated a long wait but we were lucky that it filled quickly and we were off. A conductor came round for the fares but Duncan had prepared us well and on telling him our destination we gave him the precise amount to avoid the complication of getting change which always seems to be a problem. We were the only white faces on the bus and the announcement of our destination seemed to cause some surprise to other passengers for Tera Emni is very small. But they were all smiles and clearly wanted to ask us questions which were frustrating for all because we could not say more than a few basic Tigrinya expressions.

Nevertheless they seemed pleased that we should want to go there and at the end of our journey we had no fear of missing the stop for there was a chorus of voices and hand signals to tell us of our arrival. On getting off the bus we met Duncan quite by chance. He was on his bicycle and was setting off to get some much needed water. It had not rained in the village since our departure and Duncan's water barrel was empty so it was clear that the rainy season had at last ended and there stretched before them a six month dry season. We began to walk to his house while he set off in the direction of the well, but we had not gone far when our bags were once again taken by the children who seemed to enjoy our arrivals. Not once did we ever need to carry anything into the house on our various visits there. Duncan returned some time later with the water having been unsuccessful at the well because of the broken pump. He had to go further to where a farmer was pumping irrigation water onto his land to fill his jerry can. Later that evening we had a surprise visit from one of the daughters of the next door neighbour, a young girl of about 9, who was carrying a full 20 litre jerry can of water in a sling on her back. Duncan was very moved by this gift and inevitably made the traditional refusal of it several tines before he finally agreed to accept it. It seems that what had prompted this gift was that the previous day the girl had come to him upset that her widowed father had gone to Asmara leaving her in the care of her grandmother, but he had not left her an exercise book for her to go to school with. Duncan had no book but had given her the money to buy one but her gift was far greater than his gift. The next day she came round again with her brothers and sisters and we took the opportunity of giving them some sweets which we had brought with us from England which received a bright reception. Duncan hoped that this would not set up yet another obligation which she would seek to repay!

That evening we had an invitation to eat at the house of Birhane the village Pharmacist and his wife Genet who is the village nurse. Their house is right in the middle of the main part of the village on the main road. It was dark when we arrived and the room was lit by a single oil-lamp and it took some time for one's eyes to become familiar with the gloom. What we had not realised was that Genet was ill and was lying in her bed in the centre of the room. She seemed pleased at our arrival and sat up talking quietly and said she had indigestion. This was clearly not the case for she had spent some three weeks previously in bed and had only had a few days remission before having a relapse that very day. It seems hard for us to realise that here was a nurse, the wife of a pharmacist, who clearly had not consulted a doctor (perhaps because of the expense) and whose illness was therefore undiagnosed. It seems that it is quite customary for the sick to take part in social events (perhaps to cheer them up), but also that they might see guests perhaps for the last time. Terrible thought.

The meal was served totally by her daughter although Genet was not able to eat. Our meal was very similar to those we had already partaken because what we were served was the best that they could provide and we were considered honoured guests. It was a responsibility we tried hard to live up to.

I need to say here that several months later when we were home, we received a letter from Duncan to say that Genet appeared to have fully recovered her health. It seemed to be a miracle.

We walked home later by the light of our torches. There was no moon and the absolutely pitch black darkness made the stars visible in a way that I had never before experienced. These were so bright that they seemed lower in the sky. The Milky Way was particularly visible covering a large part of the sky. In the distant hills we could see frequent lightening so presumably someone was getting rain, but this was the only light we could see except for an occasional vehicle on the road. As we arrived at the gate to his garden I did see a further light about a mile distant. Duncan explained that this was the modern hotel that was being built a little outside the village. I thought he was joking but he was not as I explain later.

We spent most of our last week in Eritrea living in Duncan's house in Tera Emni. During that time Duncan was very busy in preparation for school and had to attend each morning to assist with registration of pupils for the new scholastic year. In England this is mostly arranged at the end of the previous term but in Eritrea they cannot register until they know precisely how many they can take. One problem was the huge numbers needing education and another is the potential for teachers to leave either the district or the profession. Wages are very low and had been held the same since Independence some five years earlier and there had been unrest in the profession because of the extreme pressures of dealing with very large classes in poor conditions. A whole week was set aside for registration during which some 1200 pupils applied and 1050 were accepted on the basis of about 50-60 pupils per class. One hundred and fifty were told to look elsewhere but it was known that they would have problems finding any school. When I asked Duncan how they selected those to reject he said that sadly they hold a ballot rather than use an entrance test which would be too expensive to administer. Those children who are accepted walk to and from school each day from as far afield as 7-8 miles.

We had brought with us a large bag of books which were a present from Hollington Infants' School in Hastings and one day we went to the school to see it for ourselves and to present our gift. We were somewhat disappointed that although the pupils were required to come to school each day, no school classes were being held during our final week. We saw the headmaster, Kahsay, who thanked us and told Duncan to arrange for us to meet his class of the previous year. The purpose of this was for them to ask Jan and I questions as it would be good for them to practice their English. They all assembled in one of the class buildings which were all low single storey blocks built in rows. We were greeted by a sea of smiling black faces sitting mostly at desks in formal rows, but some had no desks and sat on large stones. As we came in the door we were surprised that all the children stood up. We started by telling them a little about ourselves and then we invited questions. They were a little shy at first but when we complimented them on their English it broke the ice somewhat. They all had a rather grand and fixed idea of what life in England was like and we tried to explain the truth carefully. It was a poignant experience and our only regret was that we could not observe them at lessons.

The class reading books we had brought from England

On another day whilst Duncan was at school we decided to take a walk round Tera Emni to take some photographs. A walk round the village may sound very mild for what was in fact a very rugged walk. A large part of Tera Emni is built literally round a large hill and was much bigger than we had imagined. Away from the main road it was mostly farmhouses largely thatch roofed and built from the local stone of which there was an overabundance. It was very steep in places and rocky all the way so we made slow progress, especially as the temperature was about 80F degrees. We met many people with whom we exchanged "Salaams" and on one occasion we met two women herding cattle along a rocky path and I ventured to say "Salamat kamelhakee" which was the equivalent of "hello how are you" and was the limit of my knowledge of Tigrinya greetings. However they guessed who we were, for Duncan is obviously well known in the village, and also knowing he speaks Tigrinya well assumed I did also. What followed was hilarious because I could not understand a word of her torrent of language and we all laughed at the joke. In sign language we were invited to come for a drink at their home but we had to decline as we knew that the coffee ceremony would take at least an hour and we could only communicate in gestures and facial expressions. We knew also that they could probably not afford to entertain us, for food would have to be provided too. We declined with exaggerated facial expressions of regret, shook hands and parted wreathed in smiles. At the edge of the village we came upon the hotel whose lights we had seen previously and we were able to wander around it. This is going to be either a large white elephant or an inspired investment. It will be a modern hotel when completed with en-suite bathrooms, a swimming pool and electricity produced by a generator. This in a village without electricity and with water problems!

Later as we passed houses we saw many children and we were as much objects of curiosity as we were curious to see them. Often we could see a row of faces one above the other looking round their doorways and when we waved sometimes it was returned but often their shyness got the better of them and they disappeared. I met a young boy playing with a football that was once inflatable but now was punctured but it still served to kick around and we played together for a little while. Later after our trek we made our way back to the main road having decided to catch a bus to Mendefera for some provisions and also to pick up any mail there might be for Duncan. The bus stop is right outside Yosef's bar which was a grand name for a blue tarpaulin tent draped over supports in front of Yosef's house. We were very thirsty and asked for two sprite lemonades and sat in the shade enjoying the refreshment. Duncan had previously introduced us to "Josie" as he is generally known and so we chatted for a while. He was about 70 years old and had fought in the British army against the Italians during the Second World War and had later been a fighter in the 30 year war of independence from Ethiopia. Having been both a soldier and a teacher for a large part of his life, he was now officially retired but the bar was a means of eking out his pension. He spoke English well and also spoke Italian, Tigrinya, Arabic, Swahili and another local language from Kenya. He was clearly a wise old man for when we asked him about Isaias Afwerki the President he would not, as many had done, praise him unconditionally but just said "wait and see". He told us stories of his own exploits and he was in full flow when we heard the bus hooting to let people know of its arrival. We just could not interrupt him it would have been impolite so we let the bus go. When we did decide to leave he would not accept payment for the drinks and I could not press money on him so I compromised and offered to take his photograph and send him a copy from England on our return. This clearly pleased him but instead of letting me take a photo of him sitting in his armchair relaxed and smiling, he insisted on going outside and put on a solemn face as is apparently customary in Eritrea. As we shook hands he asked us if we would write to him and we promised we would.

We walked a little way outside the village and then decided to hitch-hike. It is quite customary for people to do this and we had given many lifts ourselves when we had a hired car. The first vehicle that came along stopped for us and the driver said in good English that he was only going to Mendefera which was our destination. He told us he was building a new restaurant in the high street and by Eritrean standards he was very rich. By car the journey was less than 15 minutes and we were soon dropped in the town centre. We made our way to the Post Office and there met Daniel who sorts the mail. We did not need to introduce ourselves because he already knew who we were and straight away opened the PO Box and gave us a single letter for Duncan. So this is how Duncan gets his letters we thought but we later found out that Daniel frequently cycles to Tera Emni to give Duncan a personal service.

After making some purchases in the market we went to the restaurant in the main hotel for a meal which was a little out of town in the opposite direction from where we had come. We had barely started eating when who should come in but Duncan. It was his lunch hour from school and he had needed a book from his house but on arrival could not get in because we were out and I had his key. As it was important he decided to look for us. Now we had not expected Duncan to come home and so we had not told him of our intentions so we were puzzled as to how he found us on the far side of a town which was more than 10 miles away from Tera Emni. "Oh it was simple" he said, "I just asked in the village and was told you had been seen hitching towards Mendefera, so I also hitched a lift and when I arrived here I kept asking after two elderly white people and was able to follow your trail to the Post Office, the market, and then out here". I may have mentioned before that it was impossible for us to be anonymous in Eritrea but here was proof of just how conspicuous we obviously were. Duncan immediately left to go back to school whilst we finished our meal before once again hitching back to Duncan's house in a car whose driver spoke no English but who recognised the name "Tera Emni".

That evening we went for a meal at Nigisti's compound. She was a widow but she owned enough land to have a compound in which there were several houses which she rented out, and were occupied by some of Duncan's colleagues at school. It was dark on arrival and again the interior was lit by only a single lamp. Nigisti was a very lively woman in her fifties who welcomed us in Tigrinya (translated by Girmai who was also there) whilst her daughters served the now familiar injera meal. One thing that I noted which surprised me was that her status was such that she had a TV in the room despite the fact that the village had no electricity. It apparently was run from a car battery. When the meal was finished we were asked if we minded that they watched it and of course we agreed. At that the set was lifted towards the door and turned round so that it faced outwards. We were then asked to come outside and to our surprise we could make out a ring of faces sitting in a semi-circle in the compound garden who were villagers who had come to see the show. We were shown to seats at the front and Girmai explained to me that this was no ordinary programme for tonight the President Isaias Afwerki was broadcasting to the people to answer questions which he had specifically sought from the people of Eritrea. Girmai said that he was expected to make a statement about teachers' pay (and that of other civil servants) so there was keen interest around us. We watched for about a half an hour and although I understood not a word except when Girmai explained to me I was particularly interested in the demeanour of the audience around us and the audience we could see on screen. Without exception it was clear that this man was highly regarded and trusted to lead Eritrea out of their economic difficulties. We could only hope that the stability of the country would remain as it currently was and not go the way of so many African countries. We left quietly whilst he was still speaking pausing only to thank our hostess for an interesting evening.

The next morning we were invited by Elsa to watch the making of injera which she had promised she would at Nigisti's the previous evening. We found her in a little out-house which contained the mogogo (a brick oven with a built-in circular plate at the top which was the precise size of the injera) and she had already prepared the mixture. She explained that the Tef grain is ground by hand and mixed with water until looking something like a batter and then left for three days to ferment. We were to witness the final stage of the process for she had stoked the wood fire until the plate was of the required temperature and then she slowly poured the mixture onto the plate in a circular motion until it filled the hot-plate completely and then she covered the mogogo with a lid. In no more than two minutes she removed the cover and we could see the mixture had turned into the familiar greyish pancake about 20 inches in diameter covered in tiny bubble holes from the fermenting process. This she carefully scooped up and placed flat in a very large muslin lined woven basket and then covered it with a similarly fashioned lid. She repeated this process many times until she had a stack of injera which she finally covered with yet more muslin before replacing the lid. This was several days' supply and I knew that Duncan would be getting his share of these later. Whilst she was cooking she was joined by Freweini, another of Duncan's colleagues, who had been cooking a spicy zigny stew and we all sampled this with freshly cooked injera. With newly baked bread it tasted extra specially delicious.

That afternoon we were joined by Habtom who was to take us on our final visit to a village about two miles away called Takhita. We were to visit Abu Ande and his wife Adie Hiwet an elderly couple who farmed there and who were known to the teachers through Habtom who had been their son's teacher. Apparently Duncan and his colleagues went there regularly and had enjoyable social occasions in their home and Duncan had been instructed to bring his parents with him the next visit. There is no road to Takhita and so we walked across country for half an hour before we arrived at their farm-house which was surrounded by a stout wooden fence forming a compound. On arrival we were met by Adie Hiwet dressed in traditional dress with a shawl over her head and we were startled by the high pitched ululation which she gave as she raced forward and hugged and kissed first my wife and then myself. She was so excited that it became infectious and everyone was talking with great animation but none more so than Adie Hiwet. Jan could not suppress the tears as she thanked her for the welcome (we could not understand a word she said yet we understood everything) as we were waved across the threshold. For a 60 year old she was extremely nimble and when we were seated she raced about preparing a fire to make coffee talking animatedly all the while. The house was one of the largest we had been in for its thatched roof was supported by enormous beams and supports which were in fact sizeable tree trunks (the house must have been old because such trees just did not exist any longer in Eritrea). It was divided into two portions by a white painted baked mud wall; we were sitting in the common area whilst the rear comprised the sleeping quarters for the couple and their family. The floor was compacted clay covered in straw, and hens and chicks scuttled around looking for food. Also inside were a small goat and a cat. The high threshold we had crossed kept outside a large ox which nevertheless looked into the room to see what was going on. It was a scene which would not have been out of place in biblical times and Jan said to me that if Joseph and Mary had looked in and asked for lodgings she would not have been surprised. Abu Ande was quiet by comparison with his wife and he was also traditionally dressed and looking much like the shepherd that he was with crook and all. To our surprise we were given a sumptuous meal not just coffee and we all talked for a long while with Habtom and Duncan doing the translation. We stayed so long that it was dark before we left and then we realised that we had no torches having expected only to stay an hour or so. It would have been quite difficult for us to walk over such difficult terrain in the pitch darkness and so Adie Hiwet rushed out and returned ten minutes later with a torch she had borrowed from a neighbour. Once again there was an emotional farewell and we promised we would write to them and send copies of the photographs we had taken. I am not sure how Habtom was able to find his way back to Tera Emni but we made it without mishap.

An injera meal in the home of Abu Ande and Ade Huwet

That evening all of Duncan's friends came round for coffee, this time made by Freweini, to give us a final send-off because we were to leave next day. It was during this evening that it occurred to us just how hard it would be to leave these lovely, dignified yet emotional people, and Duncan caught the mood too for he suddenly realised that it would be even worse for him when his turn came to leave in the summer of 1997.

But leave we did the next day hitching with Duncan to Asmara before flying early the following day from Asmara Airport. We were sad to leave him and we certainly now understood why he had become so attached to the people of Eritrea. He looked wistful as he waved us goodbye and it was not a surprise when we discovered in the next letter we received from him in England that he had decided to stay on a further year. In later weeks we also received a letter from him telling us that he had formed a relationship with the girl we had noticed in the new VSO contingent in Asmara. Her name was Barbara, her parents were from Jamaica and she was a little older that him. She had formerly been a deputy head at a London School. He seemed very much taken with her.

A little while later Barbara had to come to England to see her new grandson, Shakeem. Her daughter, Chantelle, had asked her to return permanently but Barbara had refused, but she needed to see the new baby. Whilst in England she contacted us to ask if she could stay a while with us and we were very pleased to agree, being partly intrigued. We enjoyed her lively company anyway, but when she asked if she could see photographs of Duncan when he was younger, we realised that the two of them were serious about each other. Her home was in Luton, so I wondered how it was that she had been a Deputy Head in a London school, but it seemed that she just commuted each day. When I asked which school she worked at I was astounded that it was Queen's Park Primary, the school which I had attended as a child 50 years previously (although it was then called Droop Street Primary)..

What a fantastic coincidence!! We then tried to discover the people we each knew, but at such a distance of time there was only one person, Mr. Vater. He had been my form master and also the sports master who ran the school football team (of which I was a member). He had become the headmaster at some stage but had since retired, although he still visited the school.

I could barely believe that of all the hundreds of primary schools there are in London, we had shared the same one. I was beginning to think spooky thoughts of destiny!

Some months later we discovered that Barbara had gone to the same Teacher Training College as Duncan's brother's wife Jane, which certainly nailed the destiny theory.

ERITREA PART 2

We were not surprised that Duncan had decided to extend his tour in Eritrea. We were surprised though, when in early 1998 he asked us if we would like to come out again. We needed no second invitation because we had been so captivated by the people of Eritrea. He particularly wanted us to come in February to help him celebrate his 30th birthday although we had originally suggested a visit in May - how grateful we were that we changed this, for by May a war had started!

We flew out just a few days before Duncan's big day in February so we were able to witness just how Eritreans celebrate (for Duncan wanted it to be totally Eritrean in style). We spent a few days in the capital Asmara meeting old friends both VSO and Eritrean. During this time we made some new friends and received invitations to eat at the home of a Moslem family, and also to visit a kindergarten (Jan is an Infant Teacher and especially loved this visit). We ate in several of the cafes and restaurants we remembered and noted how much had been done to improve the city in terms of redecorated buildings and renewed roads and pavements as the hardworking Eritreans continued to rebuild their city. Duncan was working in Asmara having left his teaching job in Tera Emni and was still working hard himself so we only saw him in snatches initially. He had two main jobs, his official one was as an employee of the Eritrean Government, to train Eritrean teachers the methodology of teaching English; but he had also started an unofficial task to improve the material which they used to teach. Our subsequent involvement in this task was to prove a memorable experience for Jan and I, but more of that later.

Duncan's party was to be held in Tera Emni the village where he had taught for two years, which was for him his spiritual home in Eritrea. We travelled down the previous day by hired car, about an hour's drive over well maintained roads. The village is south of the capital on the main thoroughfare to Ethiopia and we noted that there was more traffic on the roads than previously. There were really more animals in the fields too - mixed herds of cattle, sheep, goats and donkeys - but this was the dry season and later these same fields would be planted with crops and the animals excluded.

We had booked to stay in the Green Island Hotel on the outskirts of the village, which for us starkly contrasted with our previous visit to Tera Emni. Then we stayed in Duncan's house which, like all the houses in the village, was without electricity and sanitation, and water was a precious commodity which had to be fetched from a well. The hotel (which we had seen under construction a year earlier in 1996) was now complete and boasted mains electricity by virtue of its own generator, rooms with showers and toilets en suite, and would you believe it, a swimming pool. This was only the second swimming pool to be built in the entire country, the other being in Asmara. Although the hotel provided a valuable source of employment to local people, we wondered how such a hotel could exist in an agricultural community and so far from towns. It seemed that it did attract richer Eritreans and the occasional business man; it would be a tourist attraction too if tourism in Eritrea were ever to take off.

We used the hotel as our base for the next two days, mostly sitting in the shade offered by buildings round the pool, and our party gradually increased in number as Duncan's VSO friends slowly arrived. But there was work to be done to prepare for the party and we did not want to miss any of the preparations. It was to be a community affair with about 60 or 70 people expected to turn up and Duncan had permission to use the school room for the event. He went first of all through the village with the prime aim of asking selected people to help with the cooking and preparation of food for the party. Now as he was only an infrequent visitor to the village he was inevitably engaged in long conversations before he could move on. Eventually we got in the car to go to the nearest town, Mendafera, about 10 miles further south together with two of his former colleagues Habtom and Fitsum. These two had been our constant companions on our previous visit, and as they spoke good English they were good company.

The market was in full swing and our first task was to purchase fruit and vegetables. This involved visiting various stalls, the owners of which were all known to Duncan and his friends and involved much greeting, and «bumping», (the peculiar way men have of greeting).

Next we needed to purchase a large flagon of the local brew, a sort of home made beer made from a local grain called Tef, which gloried in the name of Suwa. This is always made by women in their own homes, but it is a recognised business. There are two varieties, the better one being fermented for longer, and it was this that we sought. The houses which sold Suwa put out flags of red or green depending on the variety. We looked for the red flag of a woman who was reputed to make the finest in the town. As we entered the dark interior of her house I noticed that the flag was nothing more than a little girl's dress. We sat down and were offered bread to eat and then we each tasted the lady's brew. Now my previous experience of Suwa was not of the best, but I was delighted to find that this one was excellent – Fitsum certainly knew where to come. The purchase was quickly agreed and a large plastic jerry can was filled, which we put in the car with our other purchases.

The last stop was to a field on the edge of town where live animals could be purchased. As was the custom at a celebration, the host provides meat and in this case it was to be a sheep. Meat is by no means an everyday food in Eritrea and as there is little refrigeration and the country is hot, animals are purchased live, killed at the required time, and the meat eaten soon after. The animals were tethered in groups close to the farmer who was selling, and Habtom approached a group, examined a sheep carefully, he haggled a price with the farmer but rejected the price offered. He did this with several farmers and he looked most expert in his dealings, but afterwards I learned that he knew very little about animals and what he was doing was just an act to bid the asking price down. Eventually one was purchased and Fitsum put a rope around it and led it back to the car, quipping that he had a "licence to drive a sheep". It sounded funnier because he pronounced "sheep" as "ship" Next the poor animal had all four legs trussed and put in the boot of the car with the lid open to drive back to Tera Emni which we did straight away We stopped at the school first to offload the Suwa, then stopped at various houses giving fruit and vegetables to those who had agreed to prepare dishes. Fitsum then took the sheep to a piece of waste ground and there he slaughtered the animal (just before this Jan had tactfully returned to the hotel). It is part of the ethnic upbringing in this part of the world that a man should be skilled in this, and in cutting up meat. He and Habtom quickly reduced it to a carcase, but, as almost nothing is wasted, they cleaned and laid out on a large injera dish all the offal which was later delivered to various houses to be made into dishes. The carcase itself was delivered to the kitchen of the hotel where it too would be cut up and cooked. The sheep's skin was cleaned and would be later sold and the only unusable part of the animal were the hoofs There was one last call to make and we drove the car to a local bar where crates of beer were purchased and then taken to the school.

We returned to the hotel, but before it was dark we got ourselves ready and made our way to the school to prepare the room. We had brought with us a few decorations and balloons to hang, but this proved to be more difficult than anticipated as we had to bang nails into the very hard walls with a stone for lack of a hammer, and this mostly by torchlight as it had become quite dark by then. The rough walls also caused many balloons to burst but we eventually succeeded and had just finished when someone came in with a hurricane lamp and candles and we could then see our efforts properly. In one corner a small bar was set up and manned by Eric from the Peace Corps (the American equivalent of VSO) who worked in the village; in another had been set up the "disco" which consisted of a portable battery-operated stereo and some cassette tapes. Our disc jockey was to be Habtab, a huge man, unusual in Eritrea, whom we nicknamed the gentle giant. Progressively the tables which had been set up in the centre of the room were filled with dishes of food as the villagers brought them in one by one. Duncan had earlier ordered injera when we were in Mendafera and he had gone back there in the car to fetch it. He then came in with a huge basket filled with freshly baked injera which is used as a means of scooping up food from a plate. Now all was complete and as I surveyed the tables there were more dishes than I had ever seen in Eritrea, but it was difficult to see what they were due to the dim light. But we were to discover that without exception they were all excellent. The large flat injera (like huge 2 foot wide pancakes) were rolled and then cut into sections like swiss rolls, and we all had individual plates this time (normally food is eaten on a huge communal plate).

Jan and I, having taken our fill from the tables enjoyed what we ate but then found that we were continually plied with refills by the women from the village. We slowly came to realise our status in the company, for after this we were not allowed to fetch anything for ourselves. In Africa, older people are venerated, and parents are venerated, but not only were we both but we were the parents of Duncan, in whose honour this party was given so we became special in their eyes, a little to our embarrassment. When everyone had eaten their fill there was still a lot of food left, and this was removed to the next room to be distributed to villagers next day, for nothing is ever wasted.

The centre of the room was then cleared for dancing and Habtab did a marvellous job of ensuring that there was a continual selection of music to please the multicultural assembly. There was Eritrean music, European or American dance music and even Ethiopian and Sudanese. One dance was the Macarena, a Western dance, where we had to learn the moves which called for people to jump and do a half turn at each chorus. Jan had teamed up with Barbara to dance but as we turned, Barbara's extremely long hair continually gave people a whack. This caused a lot of laughter.

We felt obliged to join in the Eritrean traditional dancing, much to the obvious delight of those present. Fortunately it is quite slow and rhythmic but with intricate footwork which we vainly tried to copy, but we were more successful with the simultaneous body swaying and shoulder rolling which we were able to copy from those around us. At first we slowly progressed round the room in a circle but then the beat changed and the progression stopped and people paired up facing each other (usually men with men and women with women). The movements also changed but this was an opportunity to copy in mirror image fashion what the person opposite was doing. In this arms are raised above heads, one turns sideways and then back and sometimes shoulders are rubbing and then backs. Finally as the dance ends one does some of these actions whilst slowly crouching - we found this reasonable but the getting up from the crouch nearly defeated us.

At one point the dancing paused and an Eritrean called Abu Ande (Abu means father and is a title of importance), as the oldest man present gave a speech. As it was in Tigrinya I did not understand his words at the time but Duncan explained to us later, although it was not difficult to understand his meaning. It was a speech in praise of Duncan, whom he continually referred to as "his son". This was of course a way of expressing friendship and one with which we had become familiar. Several people had made similar claims if they were older, and if not they referred to him as "their brother". Abu Ande's wife Ade Huwet (Ade means mother and is also a title of importance in the community) told us that we were Duncan's English parents whilst they were Duncan's Eritrean parents. Then there was a surprise for Duncan, because he was then presented with a marvellous set of white Eritrean Robes. This was a very great honour. I too was called on to speak (as the oldest white person present) but having been given just 2 minutes notice, I managed to get Habtom to write down a short phrase in Tigrinya for me. After a few platitudes I ended with "Nihna Eritrowyan ena" which means "we are Eritreans too". Jan later said it was my "'ich bin ein Berliner,' speech after President Kennedy. The dancing then continued until late into the night, and the last to leave were mostly Eritreans for whom parties are very infrequent. We later found out that many, being farmers, got little sleep before having to get up to attend to their animals. We returned to our hotel and not surprisingly slept late.

The next day was largely spent round the pool recovering from the exertions of the party. It was good to talk to the VSO friends of Duncan whom it had been difficult to talk to in the gloom and the noise of the party the previous night. In particular we were able to chat to Barbara who was now a person of interest to us, but by late afternoon we went back to Asmara by car.

The Eritrean currency is called the Nacfa but I had heard that it was called the Birr the same as the Ethiopian currency. When I asked about this I was told that after they had won the war it had been changed to that of the northern town of Nacfa which had held out throughout the civil war with Ethiopia. The town had never been defeated and had come to symbolise the strength and determination of Eritrea.

I wondered whether it would be possible to visit the town to see for ourselves. Duncan at that time was extremely busy but he said that we could go if he could get a vehicle and a driver for us to take us there. The opportunity arrived a little later and we planned a two day trip to the north. There was a school close to Nacfa called Tsabre and he said the VSO teachers who worked there would look after us.

We had a large land cruiser and driver and we set off full of expectation. We had previously only ventured as far north as Keren (a two hour drive) and we were told that beyond that town there was no road at all, so a 4 x4 vehicle was needed. This turned out to be only too true and it took a further 5 hours to reach Nacfa over incredibly difficult terrain. On the way we could see the barren nature of the territory and multiple examples of burnt out tanks and other military ordinance, signs of the severity of the war that had been fought here. There were no signs of any animals or birds which told its own story.

We did not go to the town but to Tsabre School, the road to which was the steepest and rockiest we had met and took a further half hour to drive. When we arrived we could see the school consisted of two sets of buildings facing each other across a central valley maybe 200metres apart. On one side were classrooms in long low buildings and on the other were teachers' rooms in a long low terrace with separate dining room/kitchens. High up on the left side were other rooms for the students' accommodation and much further down the valley was a generator building and with other services. In the centre was a steep hill on top of which was another long low block built building which was known as the white house (except it wasn't white). This was to be our sleeping accommodation which contained 12 rooms on both sides of a long corridor. When we entered we were shown into a room where there was a family of about 12 people who were sharing coffee, and we were offered a cup. Everyone was friendly but unfortunately for us nobody spoke English so we eventually were shown our room at the end of the corridor. This contained two beds and a few empty cardboard boxes as its sole contents, but there was an electric light switch courtesy of the generator. Light would be available during the hours of darkness up until 11pm and again from 5.45am until light.

Later in the day we went over to the teachers' rooms when classes were finished to meet the VSOs we had come to see. There were three, two girls Katie and Sam, and an older man Alex who was about 50 years old. They quickly made us feel at home and we sat in Katie's room to make ourselves known. They are extremely remote here in Tsabre and they only see visitors at long intervals so we were providing some "western stimulation". It was clear that the three of them like each other and get on well as a team which is really essential in such a close knit community.

We said we planned to stay two nights and would like to see some of the Eritrean underground buildings which we had been told about. Sam kindly said she had some free time the next morning and would show us the underground hospital. However, after chatting for some time, we went to the Teachers' dining room where a party was to be held. It seems that they had been expecting a former well respected colleague to come and had arranged the party in his honour. They heard late that he was unable to come but too late to stop the preparations. A goat had been killed and a large amount of beer had been purchased in Nacfa so they would hold the party anyway. We first sat down to an injera meal with goat zigny (this was very special because meat is rarely eaten at Tsabre, as lentils are the main protein eaten). We felt lucky to be included and enjoyed the meal.

Afterwards we went outside and had water poured over our hands by Sam using a jug as a scoop and then we returned inside.

A tape recorder was playing traditional Eritrean music and we all sat round for a while chatting with about 10 Eritrean teachers. Then someone got up and began to dance and we (with our Tera Emni experience behind us) also joined in and we really enjoyed ourselves. We have found generally that Eritreans get as much overt pleasure from seeing white people enjoying their culture as they do themselves so our efforts went down well. We know our efforts were appreciated because we were each presented with a 1 Nacfa note whilst we were dancing (this is a traditional way of appreciating ones dancing). As the music came to a gradual halt we finished by going down in a crouch which was fine until I tried to get up and fell over on my back to much raucous laughter. It had ended well and I had many back slaps of appreciation.

After all the fun we found that the time was getting close to 11pm when the lights would go out. This in itself was not a problem as we all had torches and lamps, but apparently the White House door would be locked from the inside at 11pm, so we made our way back there. We lay out our sleeping bags just as the lights went out, but this was just a warning and they went on again for a further five minutes. We were exhausted from the dancing and were asleep in no time.

About 4am Jan woke me up to say she could hear a noise and thought there might be a rat in the room. I got up and put on a torch to investigate the boxes in the room, but they were all empty. The noise had stopped when the light was on but resumed when I turned it off. I tried, without success, to tell her that it might be birds in the roof space, but there was nothing I could do whatever it was. We eventually went back to a fitful sleep. Next morning it was confirmed that there were rats in the roof but they were unlikely to cause any harm.

After washing with our own drinking water poured over a flannel. we went to Sam's room and had scrambled eggs which she cooked for us and Alex, all eaten from the pan and helped down with bread rolls.

We then set out on a long walk to the area where the war hospital had been established. This had been built by digging a deep pit, lining it with stones for walls, and then covering the top with wooden beams on which a woven mat had been placed. This was covered with soil in which vegetation grew giving a perfect camouflage from the air. It was a good place to locate the hospital because the surrounding hills prevented aircraft from flying low. There were several wards but in some cases the roof had collapsed. It was intriguing trying to imagine the place functioning as a hospital for the wounded. Later we were shown an extensive series of trenches lined with stones which had been the front line of battle south of the town. At this time we had a former Eritrean fighter describing for us the action that was faced here. He said that the fighters here had withstood all that the Ethiopians could hurl at them and they had seen the heaviest fighting. These trenches had been meticulously maintained as the Eritreans were justifiably proud of their part in the war. They intended that this should be a site of a National Monument. They had not only defended Nacfa, but were the springboard for the counter offensive which had won the war.

Later when we were talking with the VSO and some Eritrean teachers at Tsabre about what we had seen here we heard a terrifying story about what had happened in that area. An invading force of many thousand Ethiopians was making its way north when the Eritreans attacked and caused the force to turn back. At a narrow point on the track on their return the first vehicle was destroyed causing the rest if the convoy to be held up. This would mean that many tanks and other vehicles would fall into Eritrean hands which would make a big difference in their war. The Ethiopians, realising this, sent their Airforce to bomb the convoy to destroy the equipment and in the process killed hundreds of their own troops. It was an indication of the kind of all out war that had been fought.

One Eritrean teacher had a student in his class who had been involved in a massacre at Shi'eh. The boy wrote an essay describing his most scary moment. He said the Ethiopians had lined up all the members of his village and were systematically shooting them. He had seen all the generations of his family shot and was about to be shot himself when the Eritreans attacked and the Ethiopians ran away and he was unharmed.

Having been shocked by the war stories we were told, we finally left the area and on the way back stopped at as small wayside "coffee shop" which had been established just outside of the school. Here they served mint tea, but something which was new to me - coffee with black pepper- which I thoroughly enjoyed. We then returned to the school for lunch (using some left over meat of the previous day), after which we separated. Jan went with Sam to take part in a very vigorous exercise class which Sam had established for the young lady students. It had been going for several weeks but Sam had had to overcome the natural reserve of the ladies who had come to enjoy and fully participate in her exercises which was doing them good both physically and mentally.

I meanwhile went with Alex to his room where there were three 17 or 18 years old students. It was common for the teachers to make themselves available after school for any student who had a problem. One boy had had his exercise book partly eaten by a goat and it had to be replaced. Here we had a very stimulating discourse on a variety of subjects. When discussing religion the boys were asked how they practised it. They were all Moslem and one boy proudly said he prayed five times a day "when he was in his father's house" but this was not his practice at school. The same boy was asked about his view on alcohol (which is forbidden to Moslems) and he said that he thought it was evil and never drank it. On being asked about beer his view was quite different – he felt that beer was not alcohol! We talked about the history of Eritrea and the various countries which had dominated the country over the centuries; we then were asked to sing a song in our own language which was entered into very enthusiastically by all. One subject which confounded the boys was the physics of light, how long it took to reach us from the sun and stars. This they could not comprehend. The discussion lasted maybe two hours and only came to an end when the girls returned, but they merely joined the discussion and it might have gone on into the night had it not been for the curfew. We finally made our way back to the White House and had a similar fitful night's sleep.

The next day we said a sad goodbye to the VSO at Tsabre School. We felt we had temporarily joined their family and maybe given them some light relief from their lonely vigil at the school. They worked hard and needed a break from being on call each 24 hours.

We made our way back to Asmara, a 7 hour drive over very rough terrain, which was relieved only by the sight of a school of baboons which ran across our path. Maybe animals were beginning to return now the war had finished. I was very pleased at this.

Later that evening we had a much needed meal at a restaurant with Duncan, Barbara and 10 VSO, it was like a home-coming. We were extremely tired and did not stay to the end, leaving Duncan and Barbara to stay longer. We were physically exhausted and went to bed immediately.

It was not long after that we were due to set off on a tour of the Western Lowlands, the reason for which was to do with the work Duncan was doing. It was to be one of the greatest and most rugged journeys of my life.

Duncan had been developing, with his VSO colleague Tracy, a new curriculum for teaching English in Junior Schools. This had become a real Magnum Opus because they had found that similar material developed in the West was entirely based on Western culture and not African culture. The idea had its roots in Duncan's two years teaching in the village school in Tera Emni where he had to use what he felt was inappropriate material. They had developed a syllabus based round African culture to which students could quickly relate. Part of the work consisted of producing a huge number of ethnic drawings as features of the syllabus and they had spent the year designing and drawing it; persuading charities to fund the production, and ultimately arranging printing and collation of the finished work which consisted of two jumbo sized box files with all the material loose-leafed. When we arrived in Eritrea they were in the last stages of production and the next step was distribution to every junior school in Eritrea - a huge task. There is only a limited postal service between the larger towns in Eritrea but of course no delivery (post must be collected from the Post Office) and as the cost of even using this would have been prohibitive, the only solution was personal delivery. There was another reason for this. Duncan and Tracy felt that their new system needed to be properly explained and demonstrated to the Eritrean teachers who would ultimately use it. Fortunately the completion of the production coincided with a six monthly VSO Conference in Asrnara and they were able to both present their new work at the Conference (many of the VSOs are themselves English teachers) and also use them to both distribute and demonstrate the syllabus in their own towns and surrounding areas. This was of great assistance but it accounted for only about one third of the schools and Duncan and Tracy decided they must deliver the balance themselves, and they formed a plan to start this task in the remote villages of the West and South of the country - the lowlands.

This is where we came in. We had not seen this area before and because we also wanted to make a contribution we offered to come with them and to pay for the hire of a vehicle which would otherwise have been met from the Charities which were funding the project. The journey was to take about a week and would visit areas inhabited by different ethnic groups which we had never seen previously. It would also cover some of the most rugged country I have ever travelled over so required a 4 wheel drive vehicle. It was to be a journey which we would never forget. We very nearly didn't get started for when we went to the vehicle hire office, the 4 wheel drive vehicle which awaited us lacked a roof-rack, an essential requirement as we had a huge number of boxes to carry. We were promised another "soon" but it was more than an hour before this arrived from another garage (obviously not part of the same company for it was a really run-down looking Lada Riva). We had little choice but to take it and there was further delay whilst we drove with the owner to his garage on the far side of the city to pick up a spare petrol can - another essential item for the trip, for petrol stations were widely scattered.

It was the early afternoon before we got started, initially heading north. It was intended to travel in a large circle following the main road as far as we could for it has a reasonable surface for about one third of the total journey. We stopped first just a few miles outside of Asmara for lunch at a restaurant called Mai Sirwa. We were told that this restaurant is frequently used for Asmara wedding parties, having a verandah overlooking a beautiful garden resplendent with multi-coloured bougainvillea. There was a view of the main reservoir which supplies water to Asmara which was surrounded by trees, but beyond this the land was barren, stony and brown. The restaurant was a real oasis in this bare, dry land. We had our meal and then took photos of the gardens and views. One feature of the garden, especially made to work for us was a giant Jebena (ethnic coffee pot) which tipped and poured water into giant Finjals (coffee cups).

After this diversion we set off again and began to visit the schools in various villages along the road. Whilst Duncan and Tracy entered the schools Jan and I waited outside and we invariably became the centre of attraction for the children. We were now well away from the city and white people are rare in these communities. We used what very little language Duncan had taught us to try to communicate which always caused a great amount of giggling for they did not expect to hear their own language spoken by white people, but it soon became obvious that we could go no further than those few phrases so they just waited to see what would happen next.

Our penultimate stop was at a village called Elabored where a VSO and a Peace Corps worker shared a house (Katie and Julie respectively). We had been invited to lunch with them, but due to our late departure from Asmara this became impossible. Duncan explained our difficulties and they took it philosophically for in Africa appointments are never definite because so much can affect them. We went down to a local cafe for tea and chatted for some time. Katie was in her second year and loves the people of her village and seems well settled. Recently electricity had come to the village but ironically she did not welcome it - she has a hate of strip lighting which she can see from her own verandah and which she says spoils the night. This seemed to us to be a bit selfish since the locals would find it so useful. She told us that her father was planning an adventurous journey by shipping a 4 wheel drive vehicle to Eritrea and then attempting to drive across Africa. We were to be reminded of this information by later events. Later we moved on the short distance to the picturesque town of Keren where we planned to stay the night. This town is our favourite in all Eritrea having visited it on many occasions on our previous visit, and we spent a pleasant evening there. The only problem was the first of our difficulties with the Lada - a slow puncture which was repaired the following morning. Keren was the most northerly part of our journey and we left the next morning heading due west following the main road as it wound down the mountainside. We had soon left the mountains altogether and were at last in the lowlands. The temperature here was in the 90's and very dry and we took frequent breaks for refreshment. Again we stopped at villages to deliver box files, sometimes these were well away from the road over difficult terrain and were difficult to find. In one of these we were waiting for Duncan and Tracy as usual, surrounded by the school children, when a group of teachers came out of the school, welcomed us in their own language, bowed and then in turn kissed the hands of each of us. This was new to us and we noted that their mode of dress was different to those we had seen previously. They were virtually covered by dark coloured clothes with only their faces showing. Our next stop was Hagaz which in 1996 was beyond the furthest extent of the main road, but major road works were then in progress. Now the road was complete and extended far beyond. This in turn had caused Hagaz to grow immensely and we barely recognised it from the little halt it had been then, full of camels sheep and goats. Now there were many more buildings including a hospital, restaurants, hotels and even a garage for petrol. These had been built beyond the old town which had the effect of moving the ""centre" further west. Here we went to a school where two VSOs worked, Ed and Noel. They showed us what they had been doing in re-equipping the school library with the help of charity provided funds. We stopped long enough for a welcome cold drink before setting off for our final destination - Agordat.

A few miles from town we were diverted from the main road due to road works which continued right up to the town boundary. The works ended there and this was the last time we were to drive on made-up roads until our journey was nearly complete. We checked in at our hotel but soon went out to a local bar to meet two VSO workers, Linda and Jane, at a local bar. Night was falling fast as we entered, but as it was stiflingly hot we all sat in the garden at the rear. We sat in almost total darkness sipping ice-cold drinks, with only the light from the distant bar to see by, and met and chatted with new acquaintances that we could barely see - it was most bizarre! Catching up with the gossip is an essential part of any meeting of VSOs as this is the only way in which news is spread. On this occasion we learned that Linda had recently married an Eritrean in secret and had yet to tell VSO HQ officially. She felt, correctly, that they may have tried to discourage the match due to the problems mixed marriages presented. We all congratulated her but at that tine we could not have imagined the difficulties she would shortly face.

Agordat is the largest town in the west of Eritrea and we decided to explore it the next day before setting off on our journey. The centre is dominated by a huge pale green painted mosque, there being a large Moslem community in this area. Around it were the usual array of block-built houses and shops, but as one went out from the centre the nature of the houses became progressively poorer, changing to round thatched buildings with block walls, then clay-covered wooden walls and then finally houses with walls made of branches only with no clay covering. Although there were individual houses, most were grouped together surrounded by wooden walls which created small compounds. During this tour, Jane who was leading us around went into a compound and then into a house within. It took us some time to realise that this was where she lived. To our inevitable questions as to why she lived in such an apparently poor dwelling she pointed out that she had moved into it from a block-built house because it was so much cooler in the incredible heat of the summer (later in the year temperatures would rise to 120F degrees), but the hut felt warmer in the rainy season. We could only but agree that the interior was comfortable and cool and it made me realise that one should not judge from appearances.

Jane outside her hut

Later we walked down to the river, a misnomer if ever there was one. What greeted us was a huge expanse of sand with vegetation growing on either bank. It looked for all the world as though the tide had gone out. There may have been a time in the past when this was a major river but it was now only at best a tiny stream, and when it dried altogether the townspeople dug pits in the sand, the bottom of which filled with water into which they lowered buckets on a rope. We did not need reminding of how precious commodity water is when we saw water being sold from the backs of donkeys in the town. As we walked round we were besieged, as usual, by a group of giggling children dressed in a ragged assortment of clothes, but some were brightly coloured. To our surprise they had no fear of the camera which was not the case when we were last in Eritrea and they provided us with a beautiful memory of this exotic town. Duncan & Tracy next took us to what looked like a market, but was in fact a large covered area where different vendors were serving personally prepared coffee, Eritrean style! We found ourselves some low stools to squat upon and surrounded by dozens of locals we were served very strong black coffee laced with ginger, a regional speciality which tasted exquisite. Our tour was then over too quickly as we made our way to the vehicle to continue our journey.

After Agordat there was no surfaced road and we started to experience difficult driving conditions. It was not that the road disappeared, rather that it at times divided into multiple trails. Had we not known that there were no other roads here we might have thought we were taking the wrong route, but whichever trail we took they all merged back eventually. It was just a question of picking the least rutted or rocky direction. Driving became difficult and slow, made worse by the need to keep the windows closed to keep out the clouds of dust we were raising. We were about half way to our next destination, Berentu, when Duncan, who was driving, suddenly hit a rut which could not be avoided. There was a loud bang and we stopped abruptly. The grill at the front of the Lada had fallen off on one side only but was too heavy to tie back up temporarily. We had no tools to try to dismount the other side and so we did the only thing possible - we had to break it off. This was easier said than done, but after much wrenching forward and back the bracket finally broke and we were able to stow the grill on the roof rack. We restarted but immediately realised by the noise that our exhaust had been severed by rocks in the rut. After examination we tied it temporarily and hoped it would last to our destination.

Berentu was not just our next stop, it was to be our base for the next three days. It had special significance for Tracey too, for she had lived and taught there for the first two years of her Eritrean tour and had grown to love the area and the people. We were travelling over a bare rocky plain when slowly a line of low hills came into view, and seeing them Tracey knew she was near our destination, for Berentu is built in these hills. She became progressively more excited as we came closer, for Berentu was to her a second home and she had not been back there for a year. We climbed into the hills on a slightly better but very rocky road and were within a few hundred yards of the summit beyond which we could see the town when the vehicle stopped. At first we suspected another mechanical problem but we quickly realised that Duncan was only teasing Tracey when he calmly asked for a drink. She picked up some papers beside her and beat him over the head with them, now totally unable to suppress her excitement, and did so again when Duncan pretended that he could not restart the Lada. But we quickly mounted the rise and saw before us the low white buildings of the bustling town. It became, because of Tracey's feelings, quite an emotional entry and as we made our way down the high street, we continually stopped as she was greeted so enthusiastically by people she knew with many handshakes, hugs and kisses. Although there were many men dressed in the ubiquitous shirts and jeans many more men were dressed in white robes and the women were swathed in dresses of the brightest colours and large multi-coloured turbans, but all without exception looked happy and there was much laughter in all the greetings. I had a feeling I was going to like it here yet I had only just arrived.

Tracey was home again in a very real sense. She had returned after a year's absence to a town where she had lived and worked for two years and everyone it seemed was pleased to see her again. It took some time to make our way along the main high street and arrive at our appointed hotel which fortunately had enough rooms for us all. The hotel was tiny and all the rooms were in a single storey block lined up on one side of a dusty courtyard; entry to each was via a brightly painted metal door and the rooms contained beds, a chair, a very small table and an overhead fan. There was a window at the back but this was permanently shuttered on the outside so that when the door closed we were in near darkness except for a little sunlight entering via a metal air grille above the door. There was a light, but electricity in the town only comes on at dusk and lasts till midnight. Our room though was beautifully cool but our first requirement however was to clean up. The journey had been very hot and dusty and it was with some surprise that we were told that a shower was available. Jan was given first option and the hotel manager dressed in flowing white robes and wearing a small white round cap on his head bowed to her and said that all was ready. She was led to the rear of the courtyard and shown into a block built room with a wooden door, within which stood a large bucket of cold water and a metal cup with a handle to pour the water over oneself. Well, all of this might sound primitive but she emerged saying the "shower" was really very refreshing after the heat of the day. That night we went to bed leaving the fan on knowing it would stop at midnight by which time we were sound asleep. Before that Duncan took the Lada to the local garage and Tracey went to look up some of her friends whilst we had time to walk round the town a little, which really came to life as dusk fell and when the lights came on. We met up for a meal at a restaurant with several of Tracey's Eritrean friends who all spoke excellent English and had a lively meal before retiring to bed utterly exhausted.

The next day Jan and I had largely to ourselves as Duncan and Tracey had several schools to visit, so we explored the town for some time before it got too hot and then we spent time people-watching in bars. The town appears to be largely Moslem, especially as once again the largest building was the mosque, but we noticed some women who were dressed in bright coloured full length robes with similarly coloured head-dresses rather than the usual white. They were bigger than average, stronger looking and noticeably more animated than any Eritrean women we had seen so far, calling out to each other and laughing out loud, something that appeared to be the opposite of the norm for women here. We later were told that they belonged to the Kunama tribe who are unique in that part of Africa in that the women are totally emancipated and in some ways dominant over their men folk (I hesitate to say just like in England). This is unusual in a totally male-oriented continent, for the women are able to own land, animals and even choose their own marriage partners.

We met up with Duncan and Tracey for meals but it was not until dusk that they were able to relax again. Duncan arrived back with the Lada that evening. The front grille had been welded back on and even the exhaust was welded together (there were no replacements in this part of the world) and all this at a very small cost and done within the day. It seemed incredible service to us but is in fact the norm here. We were to eat in a Sudanese restaurant that evening but as they were Moslem and sold no alcohol, we first went to a bar before moving on to the Adul Hotel where we were served our meal sitting on tables in a dimly lit courtyard. I had never eaten Sudanese food before but when it came it was difficult to see. In the centre of the table were placed six dishes, four of meat in differently spiced sauces, one of rice and one of lentils. One did not have a knife and fork but freshly baked rolls were used to mop up the food and it was as good as anything I had eaten anywhere. One dish especially lingers on my memory, it was goats liver, sweet and succulent and we all remarked how good it was especially since we had long since given up eating liver in England. Later we met up with two more local VSO, Ian and Kate, on the veranda of a local bar. But we did not have a late night because we were to have an early morning start.

One thing that impressed me on this trip was how all the VSO volunteers seemed to be so comradely and supportive of each other. They seemed like a single family but spread over the country. Every meeting was very friendly and I realised that being in a country where each was different from the locals, brought them closer together. They all appeared to love their work and felt that they were making a difference. I found this reassuring that aid work was doing a good job.. It was good too that many had formed close relationships with Eritreans who, in some cases, appeared to join the "family"

.The next day we set off early to make a day trip to a village called Tokombia some 30 miles away - again to visit the local school. Fortunately the early part of the day was overcast and we did most of the journey before it got too hot. Once again the terrain presented some difficult driving being mostly undulating scrub land and in consequence it was hard to keep to the trail. We headed due south and thus kept on course. We started to see some wild animals including gazelle, wild camels and many types of birds and it was good to see that these were beginning to return because most wild life had been lost during the 30 years' war that ended in 1992. It was somewhat of a surprise to me when we arrived at Tokombia an hour and a half later as I had lost my sense of time. Once again Duncan and Tracey went off to the school whilst Jan and I explored the small town. There was little to see, just a few scattered dwellings, so we made our way down to the river. Just as in Barentu, the river had no water only a very large expanse of sand although we were later assured that in the rainy season this river (unlike Barentu) did flood. It was hard to imagine and as if to emphasise the point we watched as a violent sand-storm started some way downstream and slowly approached us. We ran for cover into the courtyard of a small hotel which was surrounded by a block wall, but we need not have worried as the wind suddenly changed direction and the impenetrable wall of dust moved on.

The approaching dust storm over the dry river bed

It was very hot now so we decided to stay in the shady courtyard and asked for a drink. Bottled mineral water and soft drinks are generally available in Eritrea but not here - they had run out of supplies of everything except beer and this we thought inadvisable in the heat. We dared not drink the water from the donkey back water seller so the only alternative was tea. We sat down and awaited the others.

This tiny town seemed unremarkable to us whilst we were there but it is only a few miles from the Ethiopian border and was close to where the fighting began in the war that was to break out between the two countries just two months later.

It was late afternoon before we set out and we retraced our steps of the morning, bumping our way back to Barentu, but at least the worst of the heat had passed. Our first destination was a bar to get mineral water which we quaffed greedily until we felt better, then a "shower" in our hotel before setting out to spend the carbon copy of our previous night's entertainment - another Sudanese meal at the Adal Hotel and later drinks in the veranda bar with Kate and Ian.

Barentu was in distance about the half way mark in our circular tour and the next morning we started out early heading South East to begin the longest stretch of travelling we had done in one day so far. There were four schools to visit in this remote region, all widely spaced and we had to travel through mountainous country. Ironically the worst stretch of the road was the first two hours during which I drove barely 30 miles. One had to concentrate on the track ahead continually for if one didn't the effect was to hit deep ridges at speed and risk problems. At first we passed through sandy scrub land but eventually came to a series of rocky ridges which tested the vehicle to its limits. There were a series of steep gullies to pass over with first a slow descent at a seemingly impossible angle, and then at the bottom a climb which was just as steep. To make matters worse the Lada engine decided to die whenever one ceased to accelerate (i.e. going downhill) and so I managed by coasting downhill and then virtually bump starting the engine by using the momentum of the vehicle near the bottom of the gully, then accelerating hard for the climb. The entire time one had to grip the steering wheel very hard as the track tried to wrench the wheels first one way, then another. There were times when the wheels span and I didn't think we would make it up the next hill, but somehow we did. Eventually we arrived at our first stop, Shambuko, and we made for a cafe to have breakfast.

I welcomed the break for the driving had left me exhausted. The town was not large but it is the market centre for the region and we found a lively animal market in full swing with sheep, goats, donkeys, oxen and camels for sale. It was a tremendous photo opportunity which made up for the similar market in Mendefera two weeks earlier when I had forgotten my camera. We collected the usual following of children, but found that many adult Eritreans scolded the children for being a nuisance to us, but we protested that they were fine and we were rewarded with some lovely group photographs of them

Children of Shambuko

The road after this became more distinct but still very bumpy and incredibly dusty. We were now travelling due east, parallel with the Ethiopian border, and the terrain was initially flat, then very sandy, but as we approached the mountains it became rocky. We stopped at schools in Molki and later in Arezi but we had to keep on the move if we were to reach Mendefera before night-fall. On this stretch we found there were a number of people who asked for lifts as we passed them. We only had one spare seat so many were disappointed but we helped a few. When Duncan asked them how far they were travelling the answer would invariably be 3, 4 or 5 hours meaning the number of hours they would have walked without the lift. One woman was carrying a sick baby in a sling on her back. We wondered whether she was seeking medical help for the child but it seemed she was not and that she just hoped the child would improve. Another woman was carrying a large heavy sack of grain which was deposited in the boot. She told Duncan that her own crop had been washed away by unseasonable rain and because she had no food in the house in desperation she had left her children alone at home to go to market to buy what she ought to have been selling. Her return journey would have been three hours.

After Arezi it was obvious we were travelling on recently constructed road without a top surface. It seems that Eritrea lets the contract for this work to overseas companies and because of the expense of transporting the heavy machinery, the surfacing would only be carried out when there was sufficient completed road to warrant it. We travelled all the way back to Mendefera on this road, bumpy but not dangerous as part of our journey had been. The last couple of miles were in fact on tarmac and we made our weary way in Mendefera, not to any of the schools there, but to the home of yet another VSO, Fiona, to leave the last of our boxes for Duncan and Tracey to deliver at a later date. We were now only 40 miles due South of Asmara and our circuit was all but complete. We had just 10 miles further to travel - to Tera Emni - where two weeks earlier Duncan had held his party. And yes, we made for the incredibly out of place but hugely welcoming Green Island Hotel there, where our priorities were large quantities of cold liquid, a (real) shower, clean clothes and a meal in that order.

After achieving all those things Jan and I had a very early night for our travels were beginning to catch up with us.

The next day was our penultimate day in Eritrea and, after a lazy morning by the pool we walked round the village to say our farewells to our many friends there. We had brought a number of gifts from England with us and at last we were able to give these as thanks for the hospitality we had been given there.

In many ways it was a sad day, but we decided that we must not say goodbye, only farewell and we hoped to see them again one day. It was late afternoon before we set off Northwards for the relatively short journey back to the capital Asmara. The following day we made our emotional farewells to Duncan, Tracey and others and shortly we were flying back to England. Duncan was due to return five months later in July when his third year was ended but it didn't quite finish that way.

POSTSCRIPT ON ERITREA

We returned home in from our second visit to Eritrea flushed with pleasure that our trip had been very successful. We had had no sense of anti-climax on revisiting old friends and places, and we felt that the hard-working Eritreans were at last beginning to rebuild their country into one which could stand on its own feet proudly. We wrote many letters and sent copies of photographs to lots of our friends there, both Eritrean and VSO. Duncan was not due home until August and we decided that we might be able to have a few weeks away with our caravan before he returned. We decided to go to Spain in early June, but at the end of May we started to hear reports of a border dispute between the Eritreans and the Ethiopians. On 3rd June Duncan sent us a fax to say that, as a precaution, all VSOs had been told to return to the capital, Asmara. This meant that they were away from the borders where apparently spasmodic fighting was going on. He said that there was nothing to worry about, so we imagined that it would blow over quickly. In its short life as an independent country, Eritrea had already had to defend itself from territorial claims from Yemen concerning the Hamish islands in the Red Sea; there had also been skirmishes with another neighbour, Sudan, who claimed that Eritrea was aiding the rebels in its own battle with rebel forces. These had been incidents which seemed no more than testing the resolve of the new nation to defend itself - just like a new boy at school might have to defend himself from bullies . The Eritreans were well able to defend themselves.

Because Duncan was living in Asmara and we knew we could contact him quickly by telephone, we convinced ourselves that everything would be all right. So, armed with a mobile telephone, we set off on 4th June travelling in the evening as we usually do, sailing from Dover, we spent our first night at a campsite just outside of Calais. The next morning we were travelling down the auto route and tuned the car radio to World Service just in time to hear that the Americans had announced that they were evacuating all their citizens from Eritrea because of the deteriorating situation there. This news worried us greatly because no further details were given at that point. We stopped at the next service area and immediately telephoned the VSO Headquarters in London for news. They could only confirm what we already knew, but said that there was a possibility of evacuating all British citizens. They were talking to the Americans who were taking the lead in this and we were promised a return call when decisions had been made.

At that moment we realised that our decision to go on holiday was a mistake and we decided to turn back, but initially we stayed where we were awaiting a call. After what seemed an interminable wait with no information I decided to ring the VSO office in Asmara, and was surprised when the friendly voice of Debbie the VSO Personnel Officer replied. It seemed to help somehow that I could envisage exactly where she was for we had visited that office frequently and she knew us. At that point she was organising exit visas but could give no indication of when they might be evacuated. She sounded calm and this was a great comfort. It was impossible to guess what would happen but I formed the opinion that it would take at least 24 hours to arrange. We decided to head back towards Calais but felt we had time to spend one more night in France.

We pulled off the auto route and found a campsite to stay the night and settled in. Just before 6pm (local time) we decided to sit in the car to listen to the World Service news, but as we sat there the telephone rang. It was VSO London telling us that Duncan, with other VSOs, was "on an American Air force flight to Frankfurt, Germany". We thanked the girl for the information and then turned on the radio. You can imagine our feelings to hear the news that full scale war had developed and that the Ethiopian Air force had bombed the airport at Asmara. We had such a mixture of feelings at that point. Relief that Duncan had departed, but alarm and dismay over what might be happening to the people we knew - yet above all this was a feeling of disbelief. How could two nations, amongst the poorest in the world be even contemplating entering another war?

We sat and talked for a long time. Jan then said "What exactly did VSO mean that Duncan was on a flight". Did it mean actually flying or just booked on a flight? It troubled me that I couldn't answer that question.

The next day we got up early and were soon on a ferry home, expecting to go to an airport somewhere to meet Duncan returning from Germany. But no, it was he who rang us whilst we were still on the ferry. He had not stayed in Frankfurt overnight but had caught a flight to England, arriving late, but had been met by his brother Graham. He was ringing from Graham's home in Berkshire where he had stayed that night. We were so pleased to hear he and Barbara were safe, and to know that most of the VSOs had been evacuated, although some had chosen to stay.

It was in Hastings that we met up with Duncan and Barbara, and they were to stay with us for some weeks. It was a joyful reunion, but we could see they were both in a state of shock. Their main preoccupation was that they hadn't had the chance to explain their sudden departure to their Eritrean friends who might feel they were being deserted. But as is the case when people are in shock, they couldn't stop talking about their experience and it was then that we started to learn some of the facts.

In early June all VSOs working in Eritrea had been recalled to the capital, Asmara, as a precaution, but Duncan whose work was in Asmara carried on working as far as possible. He sent us a fax to tell us this news and telling us not to worry. Although there was some news of fighting in the far South, things were calm in the capital. He felt that he might use this opportunity to go to Tera

Emni where he had lived and worked for two years, to say farewell to his many friends there. He asked at the VSO HQ for permission for he and his colleague Barbara to go, knowing they could do the return journey in half a day. Much to his annoyance they were flatly refused, because they were all on standby and could be evacuated at any time. This seemed to him, and many of his VSO friends, to be an over-reaction for they all expected the fighting not to last for long.

However, two days later, on 5th June, he was taking an English class with some Eritreans who worked at the British Council library and had told them that he was unsure whether the class could continue as he could be sent home at any time. They were incredulous and couldn't understand why. After the class he went for a drink with friends at the nearby Sunshine hotel, the newest and largest in Eritrea. They were sitting in the gardens when they heard the roar of a jet flying low over the city and then heard the sound of bombs exploding coming from the direction of the airport which was only a little way out of the city; there was also the sound of gunfire. He immediately rang the VSO office and told Saba, an Eritrean and the Personnel Officer's assistant, what he had seen and heard. Again all he got was incredulity. It then came as no surprise when he later got the message to go home, pack a bag, and then meet up at the VSO office to catch a bus to the airport that VSO had organised. Fortunately, because Duncan was within a couple of months of leaving anyway, he had little to leave behind of any value, indeed we had ourselves brought home a lot of his mementoes and equipment. Some of his colleagues were not so fortunate.

Having packed a bag Duncan made his way to the VSO office with difficulty. In the early afternoon a further air-raid on the airport had occurred and shortly after this word went round that an Ethiopian jet had been shot down, but the pilot had parachuted to safety. Now the city was alive with excited people. There was no panic, indeed an incredible sense of patriotism appeared to have united the people. At VSO HQ the mood was sombre with some in tears at the thought of leaving behind their friends and the work they were doing. I don't know if my stories of Eritrea have conveyed the feeling sufficiently but with most VSOs there is a real love between them and the Eritreans they knew and worked with. Maybe you have to be a volunteer to understand the deep feelings involved here, and for some it was a terrible wrench to be suddenly taken away, without an opportunity to explain why they were leaving or to say goodbye properly.

There were three VSO who had married Eritreans who refused to leave their spouses behind (no Eritrean would be given permission to leave at this time). All were advised to return to the UK for their own sakes and were also warned that they might forfeit any future right to a VSO paid passage back to the UK. Despite the arguments, Ken and Tessa still refused to go but Linda (whom we had met in Agordat) was pregnant and it was the advice concerning possible future problems with maternity care which finally convinced her to leave. She was, of course, in great distress. Katie from Elabored had her father with her, he having recently arrived with his personally imported 4 wheel drive vehicle. Because he was not a VSO he was not allowed to leave with them and of course Katie was very unhappy about this. They both subsequently got back to the UK after some time.

The bus to the airport took a very long time because the road was packed with vehicles and thousands of people on foot. It seems that many had decided to see the crashed Ethiopian jet for themselves at the airport. Far from being frightened they were just curious. At the airport there was high security and the American Air force was processing the papers of each evacuee. Duncan said the atmosphere was tense and emotional. No-one knew if there was to be any further bombing so everyone wanted to get going quickly. Yet the Americans were calm and deliberate and to VSO eyes seemingly excessively slow having to ensure that only properly accredited personnel were allowed to board. It seems that even in an emergency they needed to know who was paying for each passenger. It took a full two hours for the VSO contingent to get aboard the aircraft and they were surprised to see that there were a large number of American civilians already on the plane. They had been waiting there on the tarmac for all that time, and were in a highly nervous state for fear of being targets in yet another Ethiopian air-raid. On board the talk was of little else, and even when the jet eventually went for take-off, there were fears that they might be attacked in the air. In the event these fears were unwarranted and once they were well clear of Eritrean air-space they could at last begin to relax as they all headed for Germany and from there to home.

So why was it, we asked, that these two countries went to war, despite having been in a state of peaceful co-existence for several years? It was, as are so many third world disputes over ownership of land. The roots of this particular fight had its origins in the previous war which had lasted 30 years. In that war the people of Eritrea had fought for independence for their country which had been annexed by Ethiopia. In the latter years the war had become more complicated in that many Ethiopians being oppressed by their own people also fought against the terrible regime of President Mengistu. The people in the northern province of Tigray eventually joined the fight. There had ultimately been an alliance of Eritrean and Ethiopian forces against the Mengistu regime, and when victory came the new regime was well disposed towards Eritrea. For its part Eritrea allowed some of the people of Tigray to set up farms in a small border area within Eritrea and even gave them a degree of autonomy. Inevitably, Ethiopia eventually claimed this land to be their own and demanded recognition of the fact. Eritrea for its part stood by an understanding that applies to all African countries which determines that national boundaries should be those set by the colonising power that formerly controlled the country, in the case of Eritrea this was Italy. The small parcel of land in contention is in fact within the former Italian colony and so the Eritreans, to prevent a prolongation of the Ethiopian claim decided to expel the Tigray farmers from the land they thought they owned. This was immediately interpreted by Ethiopia as an invasion of their land, and fighting broke out, initially near the contentious land but quickly spread all along the border.

When the area was pointed out on a map, we realised that it was a small area of land between the Ethiopian border and Tokombia the remote town where we had made a visit just three months earlier. The area was able to be cultivated near the river, but mostly it was rocky, dusty scrub land and hardly worth going to war over. Yet it seems it is the principle that was the issue. No country should affront another by taking its land, no matter how insignificant, and these countries set a great store by not losing face in front of others.

Whatever were the rights and wrongs of the matter the war spread, and each side made incursions into the other's territory and there was much loss of life. This continued for a few weeks after the VSO evacuation but then nature came to the rescue, for the rainy season started making it near impossible to move tanks and vehicles on the poor roads without getting bogged down. The war came to a stalemate. There were other reasons for the cessation besides the weather. The Eritreans in some of their raids had hit the Ethiopians hard by destroying a large part of their Air force on the ground including supplies necessary to keep it flying. In fact neither side could afford the immense cost of such a war so the hostilities continued as a war of words. The United Nations tried to mediate, with the Secretary General, Kofi Anan, visiting both Addis Ababa and Asmara without success for their intransigence remained. Then, as often happens in the West, the media lost interest in the conflict and ceased reporting it.

So what happened after this? Well, although a state of conflict still existed between the countries, incredibly things started to improve in Eritrea. In September VSO sent out staff that was the vanguard in re-establishing their presence and aid in the country. Slowly after that VSOs who had been retained by the organisation returned to Asmara to begin again. Katie's father (who had eventually been flown out of Eritrea) returned to bring his vehicle back to the UK, having got no further than Eritrea itself. We got letters from some of the returned VSO from time to time indicating that a fragile peace existed, but there was hope that somehow things would return to where they were, eventually. And what of Duncan? His tour with VSO had finished and he continued with his plans to go back to University for his Master's degree in Project Management of Third World Project Development, which will inevitably lead to his going overseas again in the future. It gives my story a happy ending to tell you that he had one other important task to do before going back to University - he got married to Barbara. But how that came about is another story.

UPDATE ON ERITREA

The story of my two visits to Eritrea ended on a hopeful note, but that was written more than 20 years ago and I felt I needed to complete the story so far as I was able. I am afraid what followed was not a happy story because the hoped-for peace did not return, and the war restarted and ended in an overwhelming Ethiopian victory after 2 further years of fighting with much loss of life. A peace was imposed on Eritrea which, once again, had been totally ruined by the war. This had the effect of making the President, Isias Afwerki into an overbearing tyrant which is so typical of African leaders. To rebuild the country he imposed a sanction on his people not to leave the country. The National Service which had been imposed on almost everybody was made compulsory and non-time-limited. This seemed to knock the heart out of the people; a once proud nation full of patriotism, came to hate the regime and led to people seeking the only relief they could, which was to leave the country. Some of Duncan's friends wrote of the misery that the people endured. The economy had collapsed and prices soared with food becoming scarce, leaving the people on the verge of starvation. Unless you grew food yourself or had friends abroad who could let you have money you were in big trouble. Those who ultimately managed to leave the country did so illegally and usually with the help of friends overseas.

In December 2007, an estimated 4000 Eritrean troops remained in the 'demilitarized zone' with a further 120,000 along its side of the border. Ethiopia maintained 100,000 troops along its side.

In September, 2012, the Israeli 'Haaretz' newspaper published an exposé on Eritrea.

[There are over 40,000 Eritrean refugees in Israel. Eritrea has been nicknamed as the "North Korea of Africa," and is among the harshest dictatorships in the world, where limitations on freedom of movement are extreme and punishments severe. The NGO "Reporters without Borders" ranks Eritrea last among 179 countries when it comes to freedom of expression, even lower than North Korea. One of the most glaring reflections of the harshness of the regime in Asmara, the Eritrean capital, is the mandatory military service that citizens on average serve from age 18 until they are 55 and which has spurred many to flee. "Amnesty International" notes that in a country where the average life expectancy is 61 or 62, this means many spend their entire adult lives in the army, frequently facing hard labour and meagre wages. Women have fled the army because the army bars them from getting pregnant, denying them the opportunity to start a family if they remained in the Eritrean military. On the other hand, Eritrean army officers have the right to have sex with subordinate female soldiers, as it's not legally considered rape. Every month about 3,000 people flee the East African country, and there is no wonder at it.]

Every time I see people at Calais trying illegally to enter Great Britain by climbing dangerously into or even the underside of lorries or attempting a channel crossing in poorly equipped boats I realise that, for them, the dangers are so much less than what they are fleeing from. They are truly desperate people.

I am sorry to end my story, which had been so full of optimism, on so pessimistic a note but this is real life and not just a story. Two years later, when they were working in Sudan, Duncan and Barbara were able to return to see the friends they felt they had deserted and it brought closure to them to be told that the Eritreans understood why they had to leave so quickly. For them it was so sad to see how their friends were suffering and there was nothing they could do.

I do have a post-script to add which is a little happier. The man who was the deputy head master of the school where Duncan had taught, Girmai, had, with two of his daughters, escaped to Ethiopia and had been able to obtain a Green Card, which was in effect a permit to work in America. They travelled to America where he found work as a bus driver in Los Angeles and his daughters went to college there. This was to change their lives absolutely and from the money he earned he was able to support his wife and remaining seven children in Asmara and save them from starvation. When he had been in USA for 4 years he was able to naturalise as an American citizen and this gave him the right to bring his wife and several of his children over to join him and reunite the family which had been separated for so long.

Before this happened Jan and I went to Los Angeles to see him in his flat there. He actually met us at the airport in his own car which immediately showed us how he had prospered. When we knew him previously he was rather thin and did not seem to be in good health. He had very little money, walked everywhere and struggled to support his family. Here, two years later, he had put on weight, wore spectacles (thanks to American healthcare for immigrants), he wore an American baseball cap and could drive a car. It was difficult to recognise the man we knew before. He drove us home and we met Tsege and Dagmawit his two teen-age daughters. They were so eager to see us and to talk. Now they were proficient in English whereas in Asmara they were so lacking in confidence to speak English that they had said little. They were so pleased to be able to say what they were unable to say before and it was a great release for them. We had expected them to have become typical American girls, but no, they had kept to all the customs and mores of their Eritrean upbringing. We were treated to a traditional injera meal cooked by the girls, and they also treated us to the traditional coffee ceremony. The education they were receiving in America would lead to their becoming nurses and they loved their new life.

Later we went to an Eritrean bar in the town and we discovered that we were in a sort of Eritrean ghetto – where expats could relive their cultural lives. The music you heard as you entered the bar was distinctly Eritrean, and we were greeted in the friendliest manner. When one young girl was told that we knew Asmara she asked us what it was like. It came as a shock to us to hear that she had never been there! There was a real nostalgia for the country but all realised that going back was impossible whilst Isias Afwerki remained president.

We left Los Angeles feeling happy that our friends had risen above their difficulties and had prospered. It could not have been so for countless others.

RUANDA

My wife, Jan, and I experienced a trip to East Africa in 2001 where we visited four separate countries. Our prime aim was to visit our son Duncan and his wife Barbara who were both working in Kigali, the capital city of Rwanda, him for VSO (Voluntary Services Overseas) and her for ADRA (Adventist Development and Rehabilitation Agency). We were also very keen to see our grandson Julian who was three years old when they went to Rwanda but they had already been gone a year. We felt that we must see more of this region too, so we planned to visit other East African countries.

When we arrived in Rwanda they gave us a marvellous welcome at the smart but small Kigali Airport and then Duncan drove us in his vehicle to his house on the outskirts of Kigali. We were to live here for the next four weeks and so we quickly settled in. The house could not have been more contrasting to that which Duncan had lived in some years earlier when he was a volunteer in Eritrea which was then a basic block-built one-roomed dwelling without water or electricity. Here they had a large 4-bedroomed bungalow with four bathrooms, an enormous lounge and dining room plus a small kitchen and a lovely garden - such a contrast! However, a high level of security was necessary and every window was barred and the house was surrounded by a 10 feet high wall with a large metal gate that was always locked and a guard employed to watch the building at night.

Despite the apparent opulence of the house we were soon to learn we were in Africa for most evenings as it became dark we had a power cut so we had to exist on lamps and candles. Darkness falls about 6.30pm for Rwanda is near the equator and has equal day and night all year round, so the evenings seemed long as activities were curtailed without adequate light. This power problem had a knock-on effect on the water supply which depends on power to pump a supply to each house (where it is stored in a large storage tank in the garden). The contents of this slowly diminished to zero during our weeks in the house and we eventually had to have jerry cans filled from standpipes some distance away. Oh, and for good measure, the house had two telephones and neither of them worked!

Jan and I just fitted into the routine of the house, initially, which during the week consisted of Duncan or Barbara, on their way to work, taking Julian to school by car - a drive of some 20 minutes. The school was an International fee-paying school which Julian really enjoyed, even though the teaching was quite formal.

Julian (third from the left) in his small class in Kigali

When the house was clear we would breakfast on tea and toast usually supplemented by a banana or two (Rwandan bananas are very small, perhaps half the size of the ones we are familiar with, and very sweet). We would then catch a 'mutatu' or bus (a fifteen seat mini-bus service covers the whole of Kigali and runs very frequently during daylight hours) where we would shop, have a swim in the pool of the one big international hotel in Kigali, occasionally having lunch, before coming home to see Julian.

Julian's schooling, due to his age, was mornings only and he was brought home by car or occasionally by taxi with Solonge. She was his nanny, one of three Rwandan staff employed in the house. Three staff might seem pretentious but providing employment to local people was as much a part of the Western presence in Rwanda as the aid work that was done. The others were Marita, the cook, and Vincent the custodian-cum-gardener. Weekends were different in that neither Duncan and Barbara nor their staff worked and we took every opportunity of going out visiting rural parts of the country, usually where there was a lake where swimming was good. Once they combined a bit of leave with a weekend and we all travelled across the border into Uganda for a few days, again to a lakeside resort.

Well that was the basic format of our time, but we had a number of opportunities to join either Duncan or Barbara when their work took them out of Kigali to other parts of the country. We would go along for the ride whilst they went about their business, and in this way we saw quite a lot of the country except the North. Why not the North? Well, that was a troubled area on the border with the Democratic Republic of the Congo (formerly Zaire) caused by Rwandan rebels, who had fled the country after the terrible 1994 genocide, which I am sure you will already know about. These rebels were trying to return to Rwanda having been squeezed out of the Congo by a concerted effort of Congolese and Rwandan forces, and sporadic fighting just inside Rwanda was the result. Rwandan forces claimed to have the situation under control but, just like bush fire, the fighting kept breaking out elsewhere. Anyway, for us it was a no-go area. This disappointed me particularly because I had hoped to visit that area to see the endangered species of silver-backed gorillas that inhabited the forests of the North West.

The countryside is extremely beautiful, and very green, being known as the land of 1000 hills. Can you imagine a landscape full of hills about the size and colour of the English South Downs, but so many hills that they ran into each other as far as the eye could see? Unlike the Downs each hill is intensively cultivated with terracing being evident everywhere to avoid soil erosion. The country gets a high annual rainfall so the vegetation is lush (we had timed our visit just as the main rainy season was ending). Banana trees are ubiquitous, being a staple item of food, but most are green bananas which are cooked in a variety of ways, although the yellow ones are also much in evidence. They also grow maize, sorghum, and a variety of vegetables including potatoes, carrots, cabbage, onions and peppers, which for the majority of the population was the main foodstuff. Those who could afford it keep animals, and so sheep, goats and cattle can be seen from time to time, but meat is expensive and therefore not available to all. As you might expect in such a hilly country, there are also a multitude of lakes which are stocked mainly with fresh water fish Tilapia and Nile Perch, both very large fish the size of full grown salmon, and this is available to anyone who can fish.

Despite all the necessary precautions relating to the house, which were concerned largely with the potential for burglary, we at no time felt threatened by the people in Rwanda, but I would not be telling the truth if I said we enjoyed ourselves there, except insofar as we were with our family again, and this despite the beauty of the countryside. So why did we not enjoy Rwanda? The answer is the people. It was extremely hard to get to know any native Rwandan, and this applied not just to us, but to people who had worked in the country for years. Social contact is at best uneasy, and at worst non-existent. We conversed in

French almost every day with Solonge, Marita and Vincent (French and the local language of Kinyarwanda are the two official languages of Rwanda) but they would never talk about themselves and we never knew very much about their lives. Duncan had two Rwandan colleagues in his office who lived close by (one literally on the other side of the street) but he was never invited into their houses despite their accepting invitations to his.

In general they are a very unhappy race, or rather two races, for the main ethnic groups are the Hutus (about 80% of the population) and the Tutsis (about 20%). This unhappiness was caused by the strife which has been on-going between these two tribes for many years, the most recent example being in 1994 when over 1 million people (mostly Tutsis) were massacred by Hutus in a 3 month period of terror. Although there is apparent peace between these two races now, the aftermath has led to a complete lack of trust between people and has resulted (in my opinion) in a seemingly national depression where people seem reluctant to speak to each other, at least in public, leaving them inexpressive and morose. It was extremely rare to hear laughter anywhere, and even chatter among people was muted as if people were afraid of being overheard.

Two examples come to mind which might best illustrate how we perceived the people. The first was in Kigali market which is a fairly large partly covered market and selling everything from food to transistor radios. Jan and I are accustomed to wandering around third world markets and we would normally have expected to deal with a lot of requests to buy things, sometimes very persistently, often with humour but always very noisily. Here the market was quiet, yes quiet; we were invited to buy things sometimes in quiet tones but frequently by hand and facial gestures alone. In fact facial gestures seem to be the main form of formal communication.

This leads me to my second example - the buses. Most African countries I have visited have a well-developed bus system which mostly consists of a fleet of mini-buses (mutatus). They are cheap to use but are generally not well maintained and almost always cram in far more passengers than they should. Kigali was no exception and we used this type of bus almost daily to get to the city centre, a journey of about 20 minutes. In all that time we barely heard a person speak on the bus (where in other African countries there would be continual chatter). We, out of habit usually said "bon jour" to the person we sat next to and the reply would be a muted "bon jour". A direct question might get a monosyllabic answer or a gesture, and that was that. It was almost impossible to get into conversation with anyone which was a great disappointment to us. One thing which surprised us was that the conductor (usually a teen-ager whose job would normally be to attract custom and collect fares) never called out the stops and one just had to recognise where to get off. Money paid to the conductor was always done in silence, including the giving of change. If someone forgot to pay, an outstretched hand and two raised eyebrows were the only signal required. Only once, when on a long country bus ride did my wife Jan get anyone to converse. She was a young girl with a baby and it was through the baby that the conversation developed. But although I was sitting immediately in front of them, I could hear only Jan's side of the conversation as the girl spoke in hushed tones. We clearly had great sympathy for the victims of the terrible history of Rwandan conflicts, but you cannot sustain this sympathy with a people you cannot get close to.

Duncan was responsible for about 30 British volunteer teachers, and his job was to assist them both technically and pastorally. Whilst we were there he made a number of journeys to interview volunteers whose tour of duty was ending - exit interviews he called them. We, of course, were not party to these, but he told us a question he always asked was "Have you made any friends?" Invariably the answer was vehemently positive. But when he asked the supplementary "Are any of these Rwandans?" the answer was always negative. Even when volunteers lived and worked in small villages there was little social contact with the local population, and this was not for the want of trying. An invitation to visit one's, house, perhaps for a meal, might be accepted, but never reciprocated. All this says a lot about the collective suspicion and introversion of the people. The exception was the children who were, as children usually are, natural and outgoing, but one volunteer is quoted as saying "I liked my students up until they left school, and then they seemed to change!"

The people of Rwanda were so difficult to get to know and so taciturn that we did not enjoy our stay. Well, there were some exceptions to this lack of expression and emotion by Rwandans, and one of them came ironically out of a very worrying experience for us. It happened like this. There had been border fighting in the North of Rwanda where former Rwandan rebels were being pushed out of the Democratic Republic of the Congo (formerly Zaire) and were trying to return to Rwanda. Fighting had been sporadic and the Rwandan forces claimed to have the situation under control. But United Nations information differed in that they warned of a large number of infiltrators (possibly as many as 30000) who posed a serious threat in the Region and two towns at which there were VSO volunteer teachers, Gisinye and Ruhengeri, were in that area. This posed a serious problem for Duncan and he decided that he had no option but to withdraw the volunteers for their safety and rang them to say he would be coming to collect them in a pick up truck next day (a Sunday), and they were to pack up all their belongings. Unexpectedly he got an adverse reaction from the volunteers who said that they had seen and heard no trouble and having lived and worked in their town for some time didn't want to leave under such circumstances. Duncan's reaction was to say that that was exactly why they were being withdrawn, whilst the situation was quiet.

Came the day, Duncan and his Rwandan colleague Taye (the one who lived across the street) set off early in two vehicles, a Landrover and a pick-up to collect the 4 volunteers.. They seemed calm but they both admitted afterwards that they were tense. Ironically Barbara was away in Nairobi at that time attending a conference, so we had charge of little Julian. Duncan had the forethought to leave us a mobile telephone but we too were very worried about his journey. On nearing Gisenye, the more threatened of the two towns, they saw hundreds of troops in the trees at the roadside partially hidden which increased the tension they were feeling. On arrival they found the volunteers had made no moves to pack up and he had to warn them that unless they accompanied him they would in effect be resigning from VSO and would lose all the protection this gave. The argument convinced them but it took a long time for them to pack up and the tension was mounting.

Finally they all left and proceeded to Ruhengeri where they had less trouble in getting the volunteers to leave. Duncan rang us as he left this town and we could hear the relief in his voice as he said that they were out of the danger zone.

He then had to proceed to Kigali and arrange hotel accommodation for the volunteers before he could get home. It was when they arrived in Kigali that the normally taciturn Taye let out a yell of triumph and punched the air and saying "Yes, we've done it!" as a way of releasing the tension he had felt. He then said that whilst they were waiting in Gisenye he had formed a plan that should trouble have erupted he would have come back with Duncan only in his Landover, rather than let him risk the dangerous road "For your parents would have a heart attack if you were put in danger". So much for the Rwandan lack of expression, but it had taken a real problem to discover that such feelings existed.

There is a post-script to this story for on the following Tuesday, just 48 hours after their withdrawal, one of the Gisenye volunteers was on the telephone to her Director there and was told that they had heard shelling near to the town. It was only then that they accepted that Duncan had been right.

Near the end of our stay, we had occasion to see a total contrast to all this through our daughter-in law Barbara's work with ADRA. She was the project manager of a very large rebuilding and refurbishing programme of Rwandan schools and she was directing the work in 20 such schools. Many schools had inadequate premises for the number of students who needed education, and many of these were dilapidated, so a large rebuilding programme was in operation, adding many more classrooms and replacing mud and thatch buildings with sturdy brick-built ones and also replacing the inadequate toilet facilities. ADRA itself is an aid agency with a number of projects in Rwanda and elsewhere providing as well as education projects, new hospitals and medical facilities and new homes for the displaced Rwandans who had fled the country during the genocide but who had since returned.

Barbara wanted to visit several schools in Giterama province (in the South West) where the rebuilding work had been largely completed or was nearing completion, and she invited us to accompany her with some of her staff.

One objective of the journey was to take some official photos of the developments for ADRA publicity for their sponsors (in this case the Government of Denmark) and we hoped we might get some photos for ourselves for we had been virtually unable to photograph any Rwandans in our stay due to their being very camera shy.

It was to be a very long drive, for all of these schools were a long way from the main road. I should explain that Rwanda had a well-developed main road system stretching to all parts of the country, and we saw evidence of new road works in our travels, although we also saw in some places evidence of deterioration in the road surfaces caused by the tropical rains. These roads are largely good single-carriage roads connecting all the main towns. Once one leaves the main road however, there are nothing but rough tracks which weeks earlier had been muddy and treacherous (we had seen photos of heavy vehicles carrying building materials which had been bogged down to their axles where the tracks had been washed away by heavy rains).

We set off a little later in the day than planned and our first stop was in Giterama town where we had lunch. Up to this point we were travelling on good roads but 20 minutes after we left Giterama, we left the road, and we didn't return to it until after 8pm, sometime after it got dark. We travelled off-road for nearly an hour before we at last came to the first school to be visited at a village called Bethel.

This was a second-phase development which virtually doubled the size of the school. It was built on the top of a hill and the site sloped considerably. On one side of the slope there were four buildings in use already (8 classes) but the second row was well advanced and would be in use by the following term. Here we only saw a few students at some distance going into classes, so we were only able to take photos of the buildings.

Our next stop was at Nyabinyengo which again was some 30 minutes away but on this part of our journey we had to cross a large number of streams by means of makeshift wooden bridges in some cases no more than rough logs. This caused me some apprehension at first as we were in a large 4WD vehicle which must have weighed nearly 2 tons with 6 people aboard, but gradually my confidence was restored as we had no mishaps. At this school we drew up in a sort of quadrangle formed on three sides by new school buildings, two of which were in use but the third was in an advanced stage of development as new desks and blackboards were being installed. The desks were rather roughly made locally constructed ones to a traditional pattern of two to a desk with the seat an integral part of it. Children use small slates and chalk to do their work, and we could only compare this to what must have existed in British schools at the start of the 20th Century. Here we were able to see the children at work and later outside we were greeted rather shyly by a number of children, but when it was explained to them (in Kinyarwanda) that we wanted to take photos they beamed and hurriedly formed a group and we took pictures of them in front of the new buildings. Their reaction was unexpected and we took a number of groups of happy smiling faces (were we still in Rwanda?)

Children of Nyabinyengo school Ruanda

But this was nothing compared to our surprise when we reached the third school at Nyagisozi after yet another rough ride. As our vehicle approached the school we heard a squeal of excitement as only children can make, and literally hundreds of young children, all aged under 10 literally surrounded our vehicle making it difficult to descend. Our driver explained that we were "muzungus" (white people) come to see their new school, and the children responded with spontaneous applause. The excitement was genuine and they all wanted to shake hands with us which made us feel like VIPs. As we tried to walk towards the school, it was impossible to see the ground in front of us for children. I managed to say a few words to one of the teachers who spoke French and he said that we were the first white people the children had seen. As we stood, Jan could feel some little hands touching her fair hair which she didn't mind at all and in front of me I encouraged a little girl who clearly wanted to touch the white skin of my arm which fascinated her. We had great difficulty in moving around and our photos were of children not buildings and we felt totally enchanted. If only more of our stay could have been like this visit. Why was the response so different here? We can only assume that it was because we were a long way from towns and the people here were less in touch with what had unfortunately become "the norm". Even some of the teachers, but not all, were approachable and helpful. One thing we learned much later was that the school officials assumed we were the Sponsors who had provided the money for the rebuilding project. A natural mistake but not an intended one.

Our final visit to a school at Cyabakam was a total anti-climax for the school was closed and the children had all departed, but it didn't matter for our previous experience still lingered, and does even to this day. We were so glad that we had this opportunity to end our stay on a positive note.

EAST AFRICAN JOURNEYS
ZANZIBAR

When the time to leave Rwanda was approaching we were persuaded by Duncan and Barbara to change our original plan of visiting only Kenya and add a stay in Zanzibar for a few days on our way home. So we changed our flights to accompany them first to Zanzibar Island where we would all have a seaside holiday. They were both very tired after their work in Rwanda and so for them it was a relief to become tourists with no responsibilities. When we left Kigali airport they were given quite a send-off by many of their colleagues at both VSO and ADRA which included British, American, Australian and Rwandans. I think they were surprised by the size of the turnout.

We left Kigali in blazing sunshine and a short time later we were landing at Entebbe, Uganda, where they were in the middle of a tropical rainstorm. Passengers changing here would normally have walked across the airport tarmac to the terminal building, but on this occasion were met at the plane by a bus and were given umbrellas to descend the aircraft steps. Our next stop was Kilimanjaro, Tanzania, named after the 19,000 ft mountain, the largest in Africa, where we approached the airport by flying right past the magnificent mountain which rises from a flat plain. Here the temperature was 35C and the sky was cloudless as we stretched our legs during the 45 minute stop.

Then we were off to Zanzibar just off the Tanzanian coast but still part of that country. Our arrival turned out to be more eventful then we had expected. It was

124

hot as we piled into a rather dilapidated taxi; we were so crowded we had to have some of our luggage on our laps. We were not impressed that the driver's friends had to push start the taxi but further down the road we were dismayed when we were stopped by a smart policeman dressed all in white with short trousers. He wanted to inspect the vehicle and although we understood not a word of what was being said, it was clear he felt the vehicle to be unroadworthy. He asked the driver to put his gears in neutral and apply the handbrake which he did. The policeman was then able with one hand to easily push the vehicle backwards, demonstrating the uselessness of the handbrake, so he asked the driver to pull over off the road. Oh dear we all thought, we've lost our taxi, but no, the driver simply put his foot down hard (he had craftily not turned off the engine) and we were then speeding down the road. I don't know what was in the driver's mind but he got us to our hotel (at least its rear, as he refused to go round the front) and we were glad to arrive safely. What happened to him after that I have no idea!

We had booked rooms at the excellent Dhow Palace Hotel in Stone Town, the ancient capital of Zanzibar when it was an independent country, and although it looked old from the outside what a beautiful building it was inside. It had once been a privately owned house in the days when the country was ruled by the Sultan of Oman, and the Arab influence could be seen everywhere in the architecture, with ornate internal balconies overlooking a central courtyard full of colourful flowers and shrubs at the centre of which was a fountain. The corridors were full of what must have been the original furniture from 100 years previously with antique cabinets full of glassware; chaise longues; ornate casual tables; a piano and even a wind-up gramophone complete with Horn. Our rooms were huge, ornate and very comfortable, and ours curiously had not one but two four-poster beds draped with elegant silky mosquito nets. We were to be very comfortable here, especially as the experience of water coming from taps was still a novelty for us. We also had air-conditioning too, for Zanzibar is very warm and humid.

We unpacked quickly and then, having been told at reception that they had a nearby sister hotel with an open-air swimming pool, we all made our way there to cool off. The other hotel, the Tembo House, has a frontage facing the sea. The pool was surrounded on three sides by the hotel, with the fourth side open to give a lovely sea-view, but by the time we were ready to leave the pool it was already getting dark. We were able to use the hotel's facilities to change and by this time we were really hungry. We had to walk all of 20 yards to sit on the open-air terrace of the hotel's restaurant and we had a splendid meal sitting right next to the beach (where Julian later played) watching the hundreds of tiny lights out at sea as the fishermen in small boats started their work. After this we walked along the sea front to find it had come alive with dozens of traders. All their wares had been laid out on tarpaulin sheets and were lit by hurricane lamps. They were selling exclusively African artifacts, especially carvings and paintings and it was impossible to look at these without hearing "Jambo" (Welcome, in Swahili) and then being drawn into conversation with a trader who always started by asking where you were from and what your plans were. The objective of this was that if you didn't buy any goods, they might be able to introduce you to someone offering a 'tour', or transport We had just arrived, were relaxed, and didn't want to buy anything at that time so we had to refuse but although they were persistent our refusals were taken in good part and with a lot of good humour. We were already noticing the stark contrast of this behaviour from that found in Rwanda.

Having passed these traders we came upon something unexpected, dozens of stalls, all with large glowing barbecues and selling food. Much of it was sea-food, obviously fresh from the boats we had seen earlier, and there were brochettes of all kinds including vegetables and fruit. It looked delicious and they were doing brisk trade with tourists and locals alike. We were really disappointed that we had just eaten, but we feasted our eyes on the food and promised ourselves that we would return here another evening to sample their wares. Later we made our way back to our hotel having had a lovely but tiring day.

The few days we spent in Stone Town we did what all tourists do, and our days fell into a pattern of wandering the tiny lanes where the trader shops were, bargaining for artifacts to take home; swimming, sometimes at the Tembo House, but on one occasion at a local beach; taking photographs and finding nice places to eat.

The family in Stone Town Market

We did return to the sea-front barbecue stalls and enjoyed variously such delights as tuna steaks and octopus or skewers of Kingfish and King Prawns all cooked whilst we waited. We bought many items to take home as presents or for ourselves, and we always enjoyed the bargaining and the banter. Traders were eager to tell us of the quality of their goods and we learned how to tell the difference between carvings in ebony wood and mahogany - both hardwoods and heavy but ebony is naturally black right through whereas mahogany is not black but is often dyed to resemble ebony, which is of course much more expensive. On our last evening we went to see an evening of traditional dance combined with a meal of traditional foods. This was held in the open air but within the ancient fort. This fort looked as though Beau Geste may have fought in it, having a high surrounding wall with towers at each corner. Within was an irregular shaped open area formed by where internal walls had had buildings built into it. In this area we sat at table on an evening of balmy weather. We had had some tropical showers during our stay and we hoped that the night would be dry, and so it was. The dancing was to last for three hours in all, punctuated by the meal, and the troupe consisted of 6 people only, 4 women and two men. How they kept up their gyrations, swaying and movements for so long we can only guess, they must have been extremely fit. They danced at various tempos accompanied by three traditional instruments, a primitive pipe, a bongo drummer and another drummer who beat a sort of log, they too were amazing that they kept up the performance for so long, at times beating a furious rhythm. We walked slowly home through the narrow streets reflecting on what we had seen and tasted but already making plans for the next day when we would be moving on.

We had negotiated for transport to take us across the island to a beach resort. This is easily done as there are so many seeking business of this sort. We made an early start and to cross the island from West to East took us less than an hour, but the contrast between town and country was immense. Outside of Stone Town we passed through mile after mile of tropical plantations with only the occasional little settlement. At one point we were amused to find a series of "sleeping policemen" in the road and to see a road sign which read "Slow down Colobus crossing" and we read later that this was an area of forest which had been designated as a sanctuary for the endangered species of Colobus monkey. We didn't know it then but we were to learn a little more about this species later in Kenya.

We arrived at our destination, a resort which gloried in the inappropriate name of "Paje by Night" but first making sure that our transport would pick us up from here a few days later as we were a long way from anywhere. The resort consisted of a small group of brick-built but thatched roofed bungalows arranged around an amazing tropical garden. Duncan and Barbara had a two roomed bungalow to accommodate Julian whilst we chose a smaller bungalow nearby. In the centre there was a bar--cum-restaurant which was to be the centre of all our activities over the next few days (there was nothing else within miles and we had no transport). After settling in we made our way across the hundred yards or so of sand which separated us from the most magnificent beach imaginable. We gasped at the colour of the sand, almost pure white, and this in turn made the sea an incredible turquoise colour and when you saw the beach stretching away as far as the eye could see fringed with nothing but palm trees, and almost deserted, we knew why we had come.....

The next few days saw us in a sort of watery heaven. Julian could not yet swim properly but enjoyed himself endlessly in the water, being knocked over by waves and coming up laughing. He was so energetic that we took it in relays to watch over him and the water was so warm we never tired of it.

One morning I went out in a boat with a local scuba diving club, having hired some equipment, and enjoyed two dives at separate places off the reef which was a mile or so off the coast. The weather was windy and the sand on the bottom of the sea was disturbed making viewing conditions less than good, but the fish were colourful and we once saw a large manta ray with its long whip-like tail, but nothing larger than that. The following day both Jan and I went out with a dozen or so others in another boat to snorkel and to "swim with dolphins". This was the title of the trip but it was overstated for we spent a long time trying to catch a glimpse of dolphins, and when we did and entered the water, the dolphins immediately dived out of sight. On one occasion the boat travelled for several minutes alongside a family of about seven or eight dolphins gracefully leaping out of the water in unison, but we could not get close to them in the water. Nevertheless it was an exhilarating experience.

The very next day we were on the move again, and this was to be the end of our stay with Duncan, Barbara and Julian, for they were to stay a further night in Zanzibar and then to travel north to the neighbouring island of Pemba, whilst we resumed our original plans to visit Kenya before going home. Our transport duly arrived to pick us up at the appointed time and we returned to Stone Town and the Dhow Palace Hotel where they checked in and we left our luggage until the afternoon when we would catch our plane. We had organised a taxi to the airport, making sure that it was nothing like the one we had arrived in, and they all came to the airport to see us off on the last leg of our trip. As we waved goodbye to them we had firm ideas on what we wanted to do next but our plans did not work out entirely as expected.

EAST AFRICAN JOURNEYS
TANZANIA

It was dark before we took off to fly for no more than 20 minutes to land on the mainland of Tanzania, at the major port of Dar es Salaam. It was something of a disappointment that we were to stay such a short time here, for the sound of the name alone conjures up all sorts of ideas. Indeed, we had not intended to stay at all but the plane's schedule meant that it had a 12 hour stop here. For us this meant finding a taxi to take us into the city, a half hour drive, staying overnight in a hotel, then returning to the airport by 6am to catch the onward flight, all in darkness and seeing nothing of Dar es Salaam.. Catching a taxi at 5.30am in a strange city might sound a problem, but in Africa it is simple, we asked the driver of the night before if he would meet us and he did – even to the extent of arriving early and waiting for us.

The plane then retraced our outward journey to land at Kilimanjaro, but here we got off. To have stayed on the plane and return to Kigali would have meant us missing our flight connection to Nairobi, Kenya so we had an alternative plan. We would cut the corner by going by bus to the major Tanzanian city of Arusha, which was about an hour from Kilimanjaro airport. Here we would pick up a long distance bus which would take us over the border into Kenya. We had pre-booked this bus which was due to leave from outside a 5 star hotel, the Novatel, but we arrived here at 10.30am and as it didn't leave until 2pm, we decided to do something we would not attempt in England, but seems to be acceptable in Africa, we would stay at the Novatel until our bus arrived.

The uniformed commissionaire took our bags and when told we were not booking in but awaiting the bus to Nairobi, he cheerfully stowed our baggage and told us he would inform us when our bus arrived. We meanwhile availed ourselves of the amenities until just before 2pm when he returned and wheeled our baggage out to the bus where it was duly loaded on the roof! The bus was large and comfortable and left precisely at 2pm heading north along a very good road. It was a long, hot drive to the Tanzanian border with Kenya, but after about two and a half hours the bus stopped at the border check point and everyone in the bus dismounted to enter the Tanzanian Immigration Office to have our passports checked, ours to ensure our visas were valid, which were then over stamped, and we all then got back on the bus. We drove a further 50 yards to the Kenyan Immigration Office and there we purchased Visas for that country and then boarded the bus once more. We then drove another 50 yards to the car park of a restaurant where we had a 20 minute break during which we had drinks and changed some money into Kenyan shillings. After this we resumed our journey to Nairobi which took another hour and it was dusk as we pulled up in the centre of the city. We had thought that we would then have to get a taxi to our hotel, but no, the bus service had not ended, for everyone who had not already got off were asked which hotel they required and were duly driven there.

KENYA

Nairobi is a big modern city with a multitude of skyscraper buildings, so unlike much of what we had seen in Africa, but it also has a reputation of being unsafe to be out after dark especially if your skin was white, so we decided to leave our exploration until the next day, and we settled into our hotel, ate in the adjacent restaurant and had an early night.

Our plan was not to stay more than one night in Nairobi, but to go to Lake Naivasha some 40 miles to the North West, and so the next morning we telephoned our chosen hotel to confirm our booking which had been made provisionally some weeks earlier, to find that it was no longer available. We were offered another hotel on another lake but this did not fit in with our plans so we declined. We made other enquiries which led us to believe that we were going to have difficulties in getting hotel accommodation at Lake Naivasha. Feeling rather despondent we then read in our Lonely Planet Guide about the Elsamere Conservation Centre. This was not strictly a hotel, for they took only a limited number of paying guests but we liked the write-up about it and so we decided to try to book a room there. We telephoned and were lucky to get the last available room, so we felt much better. We did not realise then what a good choice we had made.

We had time to explore the centre of Nairobi for a while before sorting our luggage into a single bag for our four nights at the lake and depositing our remaining bags with the hotel reception (for a small fee). Then we got a taxi to the country bus station from where the long distance buses departed. Our taxi driver seemed concerned about us and when we arrived at the bus station he did not leave us outside as we expected but drove around in the station until he found the bus going to the town of Naivasha. He did this by asking the drivers in his own language because no bus had the destinations on display. He then took our bag and handed it to the men who were loading the bus and told us that the bus station was where many robberies had taken place and he thought we were vulnerable. We thanked him by giving him a tip and then settled down on the bus. These buses do not run to a schedule but leave the station only when full, and so we had to wait more than an hour before setting off. Once on the road however we fairly hurtled along a fine dual carriageway and arrived at the Naivasha bus station mid-afternoon under a sweltering sun. We had left behind the humidity of Zanzibar and exchanged it for the dry heat of Kenya, made more so by the altitude which at Lake Naivasha was over 6000ft above sea level, and carrying a heavy haversack, I could feel the difference. We still had some distance to travel round the lake to Elsamere and had to find the local matatu (mini-bus) station, curiously about half a mile away from the main bus station, and this we did. There was a bus ready to leave as we arrived which seemed full, however everyone squeezed up a little tighter and we levered ourselves on, and within half an hour we were at Elsamere's gates. I should explain here that Elsamere is the former home of the late Joy Adamson who, together with her husband George, became world famous for their pioneering conservation work and relationship with the lioness Elsa, as told in her book and subsequent film "Born Free". They had devoted their lives to wildlife conservation and, long after their deaths, their home Elsamere (inevitably named after Elsa) continues to be maintained as a functioning conservation centre, supported by the trust they founded.

We walked down the long drive, noting a number of buildings relating to the Conservation work done on the site. We could see other unmarked buildings but we continued on until we reached the house, Elsamere, a beautifully situated large bungalow set in magnificent gardens with well-manicured lawns. At the rear the lawn went right down to the edge of the enormous lake Naivasha. At the reception building to the side of the house we booked in and learned that we were to sleep in the bedroom which had previously been Joy Adamson's own The room was large and beautifully furnished with an en-suite bathroom, but as we settled in we were told that after one night we could move into one of the "bungalows" dotted around the site which in fact comprised the guests' rooms (the ones we had noted as we arrived). We discovered later we were in the only bedroom available in the main building and although we said we would consider a move, we liked it so much we remained there until we left.

We were soon to learn that the place was not so much a hotel as a home-stay with Tim and Renée, the married couple who ran the business, acting as host and hostess. The place looked like, and was run like an English Country House in a previous century. Breakfast and lunch were both served buffet-style to be eaten individually at tables in the long glass-fronted conservatory which faced the gardens at the rear, or if desired, actually sitting in the gardens themselves. Dinner, however, was a formal meal at 7pm, taken in the dining room with everyone present with Tim and Renée presiding and making all their guests feel really "at home". Care was taken during the day to introduce to each other, guests who were to be sitting together at dinner so that everyone was relaxed. The food was straight from Mrs. Beaton - and cooked to perfection. At 4pm tea was served in the conservatory, but at this there was a huge selection of cakes and puddings which became the fourth meal of the day!

But there was more to Elsamere than just good living. Every day a party of children from schools from all over the district was brought to the Conservation Centre, entirely at the expense of the trust, to learn about, and to take part in conservation projects. These were aimed at preserving the environment, a very necessary exercise in a place where an increasing population and commercial developments were continually putting a strain on the natural resources of the country. The resources of the centre were also made available for studies by visiting environmentalists.

In the grounds there lived a colony of Colobus monkeys, a seriously threatened species, which were supported by the centre as their natural habitat was fast diminishing. These monkeys, which we had first seen in Zanzibar, are beautiful black monkeys with white faces and white fur forming a sort of cape over their shoulders. Each day we watched food being put out for them as they were tempted out of the acacia trees at the lake's edge.

Colobus monkeys at Elsamere

Elsamere also provides food for another species of animal - the hippopotamus - which works to the benefit of the establishment too, for most nights the hippopotami emerge from the lake to feed on the grass. Those well-manicured lawns I had noted on arrival never need a lawn-mower! These enormous animals live throughout the day in the lake, but at night they emerge to crop the grass for hours at a time. Although the hippo is a herbivore and appears to be a docile animal, they are in fact very dangerous and fast moving animals responsible for more human deaths in Africa than lions or crocodiles. They present Elsamere with a problem of security for a guest which is easily overcome. The grounds are patrolled at night by guards (called Ascaris) who are experienced with such animals and who are available to escort all guests between the main building and their bungalows at night. On our very first evening at dinner, the conversation turned to hippos and Tim, at my request, took us out to Wilson, a very likeable young Ascari, to view the hippos at close quarters but from a position of security. It was unfortunately too dark for photography (the flash would have startled the animals) but we were impressed by their size, and the large number of them wandering about the garden. That same night we were woken in the night by one of these lumbering into our open window (which nevertheless was barred) and we watched them with fascination munching their way past. This was no ordinary place and we looked forward to the coming days we were to spend at Elsamere.

The day after our arrival we awoke in the room which had been Joy Adamson's own, to wonder whether our experience of hippos in the night wandering around outside our window had been a dream. It had not. They had snuffled around outside our metal screened windows eating the grass. They had not made very much noise and, after ascertaining what was happening we went back to sleep.

After a magnificent breakfast taken on the same lawn the hippos had occupied, we began to explore Elsamere. The main building comprises a large lounge-cum-dining room, a TV room, kitchens, the bedroom we were occupying, and finally a large room given over as a museum to the life and works of Joy and George Adamson. They were both very talented people and the room is full of her paintings and artifacts; memorabilia from the film "Born Free" and a range of photographs documenting their lives and work with wildlife. We already knew of the difficulties they overcame in releasing Elsa into the wild, a lion cub which they had reared themselves, but we knew little else. Whilst staying in the house we saw videos documenting their lives which gave us a greater insight.

Joy wrote the book "Born Free" which became a best seller and was turned into a film whose timing of release caught the imagination of the world and acted as a spur to world environmentalists to spread the word. Joy herself travelled the world preaching the need to preserve the natural world or lose it irrevocably, raising funds for the purpose as she did so. The making of the film influenced George's life considerably for he spent the rest of his life releasing into the wild the many lions used in the film's making (all obtained from zoos and circuses), and later many others, whilst she, being a celebrity, was continually away on lecture tours. This was a period which marked the virtual end of their marriage as they never lived together again. Earlier in her life Joy, being a very accomplished painter, had spent years painting the flowers of Africa in the greatest detail, a sort of African Keble Martin. Later she began painting the people of Africa in their traditional costumes which ultimately led to her receiving a commission to do this officially in order to document the various tribes whose traditions, and costumes, were disappearing as modernity took over. She incredibly painted some 700 such which are currently housed in a variety of museums in Africa and Europe. It seems a shame that they are not all together as a collection under one roof. Maybe one day this could happen.

Elsamere is also open to day guests and the entrance fee for them covers access to the house, especially the museum, the magnificent tea, and a showing of the film "The Joy Adamson Story".

On our first full day there we shared the TV room with a very large party of young people to watch the film. The next day we saw them again in the following circumstance. Near to Elsamere is a National Park which glories in the name of Hell's Gate. One of the reasons for our coming to Lake Naivasha was to go to this park for we had read it was one of the few such parks in Africa where one is allowed to walk or cycle.

Normally these parks are dangerous and one is only allowed to enter in a vehicle and with an authorised guide. Hell's Gate is enormous and although we thought that walking would be out of the question, we knew we could hire bicycles in the locality and so early that morning we walked to a lakeside resort called Fisherman's Camp to pick up some bikes. On arrival we were told they had only one left for hire, but if we were to wait fifteen minutes they would get another one. Whilst waiting we discovered that they had 40 bikes for hire but a party of 39 people had just taken the rest shortly before our arrival; they were the same people we had met the day before at Elsamere, and we were to meet groups of them over and over again in Hell's Gate.

We in fact waited for over an hour before an extra bike was provided but we did not waste our time. In the office we met a young man called Joseph who was a local guide. We got talking to him about another place we had plans to visit, Crescent Island, which was a wild life sanctuary in Lake Naivasha itself. He said that if you went round to the other side of the lake it was possible to walk onto the island currently due to the level of water in the lake currently being lower which created a causeway there. He offered to guide us for a full day for the equivalent of £14; we knew that we could arrange a boat to the island from Elsamere but it would cost f50 just to get there, and a guide would be extra, so when Joseph said he would arrange transport and pick us up from Elsamere we agreed to go with him two days hence.

When our bikes eventually arrived we set off along the lake road to reach the entrance to Hell's Gate Park which was 3 miles away. However, when we got to where we thought was the entrance, it turned out to be an entrance track only, and the Park Gate was a further two miles further on. This track was particularly sandy which made cycling hard work, so by the time we got to the entrance we were already tired and we had been nowhere yet. We paid our entrance fee (money which is used to aid conservation projects in the park) signed the book (for security reasons), purchased a very necessary map of the park trails, and then went in. It was particularly hot, and the hats we wore to protect us from the sun made us feel hotter still as we rode on. We had brought plenty of water and a packed lunch (provided by Elsamere) which I carried in a haversack and after a further two miles of riding we were ready for a break.

At this point there is a rock formation looking like cliffs about 150 feet high on both sides of the track and it was this formation which gave the Park its name (Hell's Gate). We stopped in some shade and had refreshments and it was here that we saw our first animals. In the rocks were dozens of animals the size of stout rabbits called rock hydrax (so the guide book said). These creatures lazed in the sun and were not shy of us as we got our cameras out. Shortly after we saw on the horizon a herd of zebra running, and we realised they would have to come fairly close to us to get through the "gate" in the rocks, and although they are extremely shy we did get some close up photos as they galloped past. This was a good start we thought, but for the rest of the day we could not get near any other animals to take reasonable photos.

We knew that we were unlikely to come across dangerous animals, for although lion and buffalo had been seen in the park, we would have been warned by the park rangers if any such were in the vicinity. But we only saw giraffe, antelope, ostriches, eagles and vultures from great distances as we were not allowed to leave the trails. We continually met groups of cyclists, our friends from Fisherman's Camp, whose experiences had been similar, and by 2pm, having travelled some 10 miles into the park (but only really penetrating a little way proportionally), we decided to retrace our tracks as we did not wish to remain there after dark. We learned later that dusk was a good time to see animals, particularly near the water holes, but we were not prepared to stay until then. We arrived back at Elsamere, tired and stiff and needing a hot bath after our exertions, as we are only occasional cyclists. Here we found Renée was waiting for us and that she and some of the other guests we had met had been quite concerned about our exploits. We were touched by this and began to realise that Elsamere was becoming more like living with friends than just a hotel.

That evening at dinner I sat next to a German guest, Ernst, whose English was excellent and we found ourselves discussing his work. He ran a local farm which produced nothing but flowers for the European market. Lake Naivasha is a major centre for this industry and all around the lake are similar farms growing every kind of flower that you might find in any florist's shop, from roses to lilies to chrysanthemums. In fact if you were to buy cut flowers from a supermarket or garage in England it is highly probable that they may have come from Lake Naivasha. England only takes a small proportion of the flowers grown and Northern Europe provides Ernst with his biggest customers, especially his home country, Germany, and Belgium, Holland and France. The penalty for all this industry is that the farms use so much water that the level of the lake, enormous though it is, is considerably reduced and has an inevitably adverse effect on the wild life around the lake. There was some general discussion about this and it was pointed out that lake levels had, over the centuries, fluctuated, and it was the vagaries of the weather which contributed to this. I can only hope this is right for I would hate to be a contributor to this problem every time I buy flowers.

We decided to have a rest day the following day, and enjoy the amenities of the house which were considerable. One highlight was that during lunch on the lawn a bold Colobus monkey galloped over the lawn to steal Jan's lunch, which had to be replaced. Later a party of the same monkeys, showing incredible agility, climbed on to the roof and tried to steal food laid out in the conservatory, but unsuccessfully. The sliding doors were then closed, but one monkey, hanging from the eaves even tried to slide the door back again.

Later we met two Irish girls who were day visitors to the house who had arrived by hired car. We got on well with them and later in the day we were invited to accompany them on a trip to other parts of the lake, which we agreed to readily.

They were good company and it was later when we got talking about hippos that they expressed the wish to see them. We were not sure about this as the hippos only arrive after all day guests have departed, but we agreed to ask Renée. She was happy to agree that they could be regarded as our guests in the house and they were duly asked to return at 9pm after dinner. They arrived, incredibly with a bottle of champagne as a present (which we shared with Renée, Tim and other guests next day). We were just the four of us in the house as all other guests had returned to their bungalows so we had a few drinks whilst waiting for the hippos. When they arrived, Wilson, our friendly Ascari, escorted them as close to a grazing hippo as he dared while we watched. They were both delighted.

I mentioned to Tim that we had agreed to go on a walking safari next day on Crescent Island with Joseph, and asked his opinion. He felt it would be a reasonable journey for us but he had a warning. He said that although we had agreed a low price for the trip he felt Joseph would ask more. This indicated what we had gleaned from talking to other guests that White Kenyans had a very low opinion of Black Kenyans. I was disappointed at this.

Next day was to be our mini safari with Joseph. He was waiting for us at the gates of Elsamere at 7.30am and we laughed when we realised that our transport to the island or at least as close to it as could be done, was the local matatu. This took us to within a mile of the causeway across to Crescent Island which contained large herds of zebra, gazelle, wildebeest and many others. Ours was a walking safari and Joseph, knowing the habits of the animals, and even imitating some of their calls, was able to get us very close to many of them, especially giraffe, which look so graceful in the wild. We were able to forget our photographic disappointments of Hell's Gate Park and indulge ourselves.

We liked Joseph a lot and before we parted at the end of the day he said he had a request. Oh dear I thought, he is going to ask for more money. Then he clarified what he wanted by saying he knew we used the Lonely Planet Guide and wondered if we would recommend him to the Guide as he might get more customers from that. I said I would (and I did) and felt relieved that Tim had been wrong. Joseph then said he would meet us next day to help us get the right bus in Naivasha town on our return to Nairobi. Part of his "after sales service" he called it. Although we didn't need such assistance we agreed to his suggestion.

That evening was to be our last at Elsamere and we felt sad to be leaving, I could not resist telling Tim that I had been asked for something by Joseph, and he laughed when he heard the request. Before we departed we exchanged addresses with some of the other guests and have kept in touch with them since.

On our departure we met Joseph, who escorted us to Naivasha, and there we met his beautiful wife who was pregnant and sat in a shady bar with cool drinks awaiting our bus. To be waved off in such a fashion seemed to be in keeping with the warm welcome we had received everywhere in Kenya and made a nice ending to our brief stay. We travelled quickly to Nairobi, retrieved our bags from the hotel where we had stayed, and then spent the rest of the evening at the classy Fairview Hotel, where we had dinner, awaiting the time for our plane home, which was at midnight. There we had time to sit and review our travels and consider plans for future travelling.

ABOUT THE AUTHOR

Born in London he served for 37 years in the British Civil Service. For the last 20 years of his service he moved to Hastings,East Sussex and after retirement he became a part time TEFL teacher teaching English to foreign students. This lasted for 10 years during which time he and his wife Jan began travelling to countries all over the world specifically seeking those which they felt had a unique culture. They started in Africa but soon their travels became world wide. They hope to continue travelling well into their dotage.

Lightning Source UK Ltd.
Milton Keynes UK
UKHW050808151020
371552UK00004B/27

9 781982 282288